Sensory Crystal Healing

Brandberg amethyst

AMARIS
Gem Sorceress

Sensory Crystal Healing

Gem Sorcery to Improve
Your Wellbeing and Mindset

WATKINS

Sensory Crystal Healing
Amaris

First published in the UK and USA in 2024 by Watkins, an imprint of
Watkins Media Limited, Unit 11, Shepperton House,
83–93 Shepperton Road, London N1 3DF
enquiries@watkinspublishing.com

Publisher: Fiona Robertson
Project Editor: Brittany Willis
Copyeditor: Sue Lascelles
Head of Design: Karen Smith
Designers: Francesca Corsini and Alice Claire Coleman
Illustrations: Alice Claire Coleman
Production: Uzma Taj

A CIP record for this book is available from the British Library

ISBN: 978-1-78678-524-4 (Paperback)
ISBN: 978-1-78678-601-2 (eBook)

1 3 5 7 9 10 8 6 4 2

Printed in China

www.watkinspublishing.com

To Selene, my dearest daughter
and fierce little moon — you've been
on this book journey with me since the
womb, bringing reflection, inspiration
and incredible growth. You magnetize the
most beautiful things into my world and
show me what it means to persevere.
Life is so much better with you in it.
Keep shining bright — I love you.

CONTENTS

INTRODUCTION

Sensory Crystal Healing is an introduction to the Gem Sorcery Method, a vibrational healing practice that utilizes crystals and a selection of other intentionally curated tools to balance the seven primary chakras, or energy centers, of the body. This practice will allow you to experience crystals in a completely new way, using sight, hearing, touch, smell and taste to create new associations and neural connections, and tap into the healing energies of the Universe. This innovative sensory approach to crystal work will ultimately help connect you with the Universal Consciousness itself, bringing you into an empowered state where you can make lasting changes in your life.

The Gem Sorcery Method focuses on the mind–body–spirit connection of your entire being. It will show you ways to establish an efficient energy flow throughout your body, creating healthy communication between the mechanisms of your physical and etheric bodies, and powerfully shifting your brain and mind to work for your highest good.

You will discover the power of crystals as tools for assisting you in healing childhood and ancestral trauma, which can perpetuate undesirable life outcomes if left unresolved. Through the healing practices of the Gem Sorcery Method, you will begin to experience how positive emotions and productive action can become second nature, making it easier for you to reap the benefits of the powerful feel-good hormones and neurotransmitters that serve your body in its quest for abundant energy and health.

And how do I know that the Gem Sorcery Method can help you in these ways? Because I used it to help heal myself . . .

MY JOURNEY

I discovered the vibrant world of gems and minerals when I was only two years old. I began collecting rocks and stones from the desert landscape where I grew up, which I then gave as gifts to my closest family and friends. Even though these rocks were unremarkable, grey and had absolutely zero sparkle, I believed them to be the most incredible specimens of earth magic I could find. As I grew older, to make them even more special, I added my own flair by painting colorful pictures on them. Then, when I was about three or four years old, the moment came when I held my first sparkling pyrite mineral, given to me by my parents. It came from an abandoned mining town and was strung on a red velvet cord. As I experienced its characteristic reflective golden light, my mind and consciousness were initiated into something far greater than I could ever have imagined. I had so many questions! Were there more rocks like this? Did different colors exist? How did the Earth do this — and why hadn't anyone told me about it before?

As a young child, I embarked on what was to become a life-long mission hunting for gems and minerals, seeking them out in desert ghost towns, gem shows and, of course, my backyard. I'd found my greatest love and wanted to learn everything I could about crystals. My collection grew in a matter of months and I was the proudest crystal collector. I did not yet know that crystals would also become the life-changing catalyst for my healing and one of my purposes in this lifetime.

As an intuitive and empath, I have always been instinctively receptive to energy, electromagnetic fields and the existence of the Universal Consciousness — even when I was a little girl, the vibratory nature of all life was apparent to me and I was joyfully receptive to it. I knew there was a spirit, or soul, that inhabited the physical body, because I spoke to the spirits of passed loved ones and served as a channel for their messages to my family. I became the bridge for their unspoken words and necessary integrations, before they dispersed as energy back into the Universe.

I still vividly remember the conversation I shared with my uncle right after he passed, asking me to let his daughters know he loved them, and to look out for them individually as they healed from his premature death in ways personal to each of them. He described how they might react and asked us as a family to guide them. Then, there were the multiple experiences I shared with my grandfather after he passed away, oftentimes to let us know he was still with us, and especially to tell my grandmother he loved her. These were special moments for me, as my grandfather and I had a really close relationship and I missed him dearly.

As the descendent of a Puerto Rican bloodline, my family taught me to explore my intuition and nurture my connection with the Divine, while also frequently exposing me to ancestral rituals for healing and divination – including the use of medicinal herbs, dance and prayer; however, it wasn't until I was diagnosed with my first chronic autoimmune illness at the age of 20 that I began deeply engaging in my own practices for healing, through the union of spirituality, mindset, lifestyle and crystals.

At the time of the onset of my illness, I was attending university, living the party life and staying up all night studying for tests. It was not long until my body began to cry out for help because of a potentially life-threatening condition. In what felt like an overnight downfall, my body began rejecting nutrients – I could not digest food, I lost 25 pounds in a span of two weeks and I was majorly depressed. I was in and out of the hospital, continuously seeking answers while caught in a hopeless downward spiral of fear and uncertainty about whether or not I would make it out alive. Several months passed before I finally received a diagnosis of ulcerative colitis and Crohn's disease. I attempted taking prescription medications for my condition and ultimately decided that the exchange of chronic illness for painful side effects was no way to live. I was determined to find a natural path that would lead me back into my healthiest and most empowered existence, and set my heart on getting to the root cause of my illness. Once I had made the difficult decision to put a pause on my education, to heal my body from the significant battle it was going through, the connection of crystals and wellness quickly settled at the forefront of my mind.

However, my journey to health still had a long way to go. Just when I thought I was getting better, new symptoms showed up out of the blue. Painful, itchy rashes covered my abdomen and the back of my head. My joints ached and swelled, sometimes rendering my hands useless due to excessive shaking and weakness. The fatigue I experienced was pervasive and, as a result, my social life dwindled – I spent a lot of time in bed, or alone in my own head. I struggled with chronic yeast infections and my bladder became ulcerated. Disassociating from my reality became a coping mechanism that reduced my pain – it helped me to ignore the responsibility I needed to take for my own healing, to get myself out of this low point of my life.

Further down the road, I was diagnosed with psoriatic arthritis and interstitial cystitis. By this point, I was tired of hearing that my illnesses were "incurable" and that I would have to accept that this was my life now — sick, depressed, isolated and feeling like a burden to my family. Deep within my soul, I knew I did not have to accept that grim reality; that it was possible to create a harmonious relationship with my body. So, I persisted on my quest to find *home* in my mind, body and spirit.

Influenced by mindfulness meditation and Buddhist spirituality, I committed to learning about and befriending my mind. By now, I recognized the foundational need for a mindset transformation in any healing and wellness practice. This is because thoughts are the seeds that form the harvest of human existence. After realizing this fact, I set off on a mission to change my mindset and plant vibrant, healthy seeds for changing my habits and creating a life I would wake up excited to live, every day.

As part of this process, I discovered a passion for neuroscience and began to understand how the brain makes, or breaks, connections that lead to patterns of behavior and, ultimately, illness. I learned that so many of my perspectives, fears and doubts stemmed from unhealed ancestral or childhood trauma, which was stored deep within my subconscious and unconscious minds. (The subconscious is where our brains store things we don't need to think about all the time, but can recall with some effort, while our unconscious is where our brain stores information that we're not aware of at all.) More importantly, I realized that those memories heavily contributed to the chronic physical and mental health ailments I battled. Equipped with this new awareness, I spent a significant portion of my healing journey exploring the deeply rooted beliefs and stories that were engrained in my brain's neural networks, facing and forgiving their origins, and then reprogramming them for success, using a variety of intentional tools — including my old friends, crystals.

As crystals took hold as a staple in my spiritual healing practice, I felt called to share the incredible wisdom they possess — the energy and messages of hundreds of millions of years of the Earth's creation stored within, ready to be accessed through meditation and direct contact with the body. By utilizing crystals to meditate on specific intentions, and create new mental and emotional associations with them based on their color, shape and density, I was able to reframe negative mental patterns and transmute energy blockages throughout my subtle body, or aura.

Crystals became anchors for the person I was choosing to be, reminding me to vibrate at the frequency of love, health, happiness and awareness whenever I made visual or physical contact with them. Not only did I start to move through deep spiritual and emotional wounds by working with crystals, but I also began to change the structure of my brain itself – breaking old neural connections and making new, improved connections through repetitive anchoring of the empowering mindsets I ascribed to the crystals when working with them.

Phantom amethyst

WHOLE BODY HEALING

During my healing journey, I felt very strongly about the importance of looking at the human experience holistically and taking all parts of our "human-ness" into consideration; the goal is not to elude this, but rather lean deeper, and further, into all the things and experiences that make us who we are. By understanding ourselves better, we understand the whole of existence better, because everything – everyone – is connected. This concept became the driving force and heart behind my work, solidifying my focus on teaching the ways the mind, body and spirit collaborate with one another, and how to work with them for optimal function and flow.

I began experimenting with tapping into the messages of the physical body, by engaging in sensory play to establish a mindful presence in the spaces specifically related to our body's subtle energy centers (also known as chakras). I visualized the physical and subtle bodies as a colorful, symbiotic network, through which energy flows in and out, delivering important communications to one another by way of the energy channels that are traditionally known as meridians.

To strengthen the transmission of information between the physical and subtle bodies, I noted a physical sense for each of the first five energy centers or chakras. Then, I created a meditation practice that utilized sensory stimuli to bring physical awareness and energy flow to each space, from the root to the throat chakra, before entering the states of universal knowing and unity consciousness in the third eye and crown, respectively.

By halting cyclical, detrimental thought patterns at their start, and replacing these with illuminating statements (which I have developed into the illuminations in this book), I began attracting the healthy, abundant life I envisioned, which further confirmed that the quality of my mindset directly correlated to the success of my healing path. My new thoughts set the stage for me to behave in new ways and create the wellness I once thought was impossible. It was at this point that the AmarisLand online community and crystal shop was born, and I began creating, solely to help people discover hope in their own healing journeys.

Over the last decade and more, I mastered how to bring my body into a healthier, higher frequency, accomplishing what many people would consider to be a miracle. Today, I am healthy, blooming and continuously adapting to the messages my body shares. Wellness is a lifelong commitment and one I am more than willing to make in order to continue serving my purpose in this lifetime.

I am here to assist others to thrive, not just survive, and to achieve this I must honor the ways my mind, body and spirit communicate how to stay in harmony and exert a positive influence. I aim to inspire people to make that same commitment to themselves, and learn how to effectively rewire their limiting constructs and identities, understand the physical mechanisms that create healing, develop a strong relationship with their intuition and be the very best versions of themselves they can be. My methods and teachings have assisted thousands of people around the world to reconstruct their lives, tune in to their bodies, actualize their manifestations, and wholly step into their inherent power. With every step forward my clients take, no matter how "big" or "small" (every baby step forward is as valuable as a leap), I am encouraged to continue following my call to share the Gem Sorcery Method with the world and witness others find the same freedom from their pain that I was able to attain.

HOW TO WORK WITH THIS BOOK

By harnessing the unique properties of crystals through the practice of Gem Sorcery, this book intends to create a safe environment for you to explore the defining moments in your life, including your childhood, that unconsciously and negatively impact you today. It will support you in overcoming any self-limiting mindsets and destructive behavioral patterns that keep you from accessing the eternal energy of the Universal Consciousness and living out your highest purpose. The exercises and guidance within these pages are designed to help you acknowledge hidden pain, release blocked energy and transmute it into free-flowing life force, or *prana*.

Our goal in the Gem Sorcery Method is to take the body out of persistent "fight or flight" mode, and to activate the parasympathetic nervous system, whereby the body shifts into a state of rest and recovery. We will be paving the way for confidence and wellbeing in your day-to-day life, and ultimately for embodying your Higher Self – the essence within you that connects to the Universal Divine itself.

While you may be tempted to dip into the book straight away at random, I would encourage you to read it first from cover to cover.

PART 1: THE ELEMENTS OF GEM SORCERY

This first part of the book will introduce you to the key elements, the context and theory of Gem Sorcery — the healing relationships that exist between crystals, chakras, colors and our wellbeing, and the role that shadow work plays in this process.

PART 2: THE PRACTICE OF GEM SORCERY

Here, we will look more closely at how to work with different types of crystals, including setting intentions with them and clearing and charging them. I will also explain how to balance your chakras with the illuminations and meditations that you will find in Part 3.

PART 3: BALANCING THE CHAKRAS WITH GEM SORCERY

In this part of the book, we will journey through the seven chakras, from root to crown, discovering the physical senses, crystals, illuminations, meditations and exercises that connect with each of them. As part of this process, I will gently guide you through your childhood, back to conception — where your ancestral DNA was coded into the thread of your being — all the way to the point before your energy merged with consciousness and created the physical being that you see when looking back at yourself in the mirror. We will be balancing the chakras with crystals to reintegrate those pieces of your energy body that are lost, or drifting apart from you, and causing states of dissociation, depression and anxiety.

By now, you are beginning to have an idea of what the Gem Sorcery Method is and the sorts of practices I will be encouraging you to adopt into your lifestyle. These are designed to help bring your vibrational energy up to the frequencies that will attract love, happiness and success to you, and strengthen your connection with your Higher Self. You are probably eager and excited to surrender to the work and watch your life change already, which is a really great starting point — keep that excitement to fuel your journey! I want to remind you, though, that each portion of this book is as essential as the next and there is absolutely no need to rush through it. In fact, I encourage you to take your time. Please read each part more than once to fully digest the information. The deeper your understanding of every concept, the more successful your integration of mind, body and spirit will be.

Reading the book and expecting your life to shift like a magic trick is not the aim here; you must take action, and employ the knowledge and practices shared in these pages. You are the one and only person who has the agency to create the reality you choose, and it is up to you how much expansion and sacred growth you achieve. The greatest power you have is the capacity for choice, and what you choose to do with the knowledge you receive from this method will determine your level of success.

Consider *Sensory Crystal Healing* a guide — a light you can look upon for influence and profound inspiration for remembering, and embodying, the you that you are meant to be. I've seen the practice of Gem Sorcery revolutionize many lives, especially my own, and I wish for you to earn that degree of freedom — freedom to be healthy, have a positive perspective, live in flow, be brave and believe in both yourself and whatever your unique intention is for walking in your most aligned vibration.

Labradorite

PART I

THE ELEMENTS OF GEM SORCERY

HEALING WITH CRYSTALS

Crystals are ancient beings, carrying the messages of creation. As human beings we are equally attuned to this energy because we are part of nature too, and when we work with crystals in our healing practice, it is much like looking into the mirror of infinite possibilities, reflecting back at us what we are capable of being, creating and achieving. Your crystals won't work unless you do — you are the power source and they are simply the vibrational tools that enable your intentions to become manifest in the world.

For millions of years, tools have supported humankind. For example, with access to tools for cutting and for hunting, it became easier for early humans to accomplish challenging tasks. Most of those primitive tools were made out of stone; it's incredible to think that we have been working closely with the stones provided by Earth since nearly the beginning of our time here. And here we are today, still working with them in a distinct way!

As tactile beings with body parts that allow us to reach, walk, feel and hold things, it makes sense that we humans have developed an advantageous relationship with tools. Our brains and physical bodies were designed to interact with the world around us in a multisensory manner, and simply by carrying a tool in our hands, our brains receive the signal that we have a better chance of successfully completing a project.

As a result, we experience an increase in confidence in our capabilities, which leads to further benefits in turn: spirit is elevated, self-worth expands, mindset positively shifts and bodily chemical processes support a decrease in stress and, thereby, a healthier immune system. With a healthier immune system, we are more capable of taking action in our day-to-day lives. Something we might take for granted, such as a handheld tool, can completely shift our perspectives, physiology and overall life experience.

THE PROPERTIES OF CRYSTALS

Because we humans perceive and collaborate with our environment in a multisensory way, this means we are impacted by texture, color, shape, energy, density and other qualities – all of which make crystals extraordinary tools for healing through mind, body and spirit integration! While crystals can be loosely defined as solids made from minerals, in which the atoms are arranged into highly ordered repeating patterns, they come in a plethora of colors, shapes, sizes and textures. In fact, think of a color, any color, and you are likely to find a sparkling expression of it within at least one type of crystal; the entire rainbow is quite literally at your fingertips.

The vibrant color varieties of crystals can be attributed to their unique chemical and mineral compositions, which either reflect or absorb certain wavelengths of light. Some crystals and minerals are idiochromatic, meaning they are always one single color, because their chemical composition is pure and always the same. However, most crystals and minerals are allochromatic, which means that they get their color from impurities or variations in their chemical composition. These impurities can be tiny amounts of other elements, such as copper, iron or manganese, which can create a range of beautiful and distinct hues.

The colors in a crystal or mineral can also be affected by environmental factors, such as the amount of heat, pressure or radiation it was exposed to during its formation. No matter the types of crystals, and whether they are idiochromatic or allochromatic, there is no denying their power as healing tools.

As well as being beautiful to look at, crystals pick up, carry and exude vibrational energy at specific frequencies. They can even pick up our energy in the form of heat, by way of conduction, when we hold them – a compelling example of the exchange that occurs when working with crystals. Interacting with their physical characteristics soothes our need for a palpable connection with our external world, while also giving us an outlet for carrying out mindfulness and metaphysical rituals that advocate for our mental, emotional, physical and spiritual wellbeing. As you will discover in more detail in Parts 2 and 3 of this book, effective crystal rituals include contact therapy (placing crystals on the body or holding them) and energy manifestation based on shape, color therapy, intention setting and programming, and clearing and charging.

You may already use crystals as tools in your healing practice, or very likely have a curiosity about their healing properties. You may have strong associations attached to certain crystals in your collection, which influence how you use them, where you take them, how you display them and what intentions you program them with. You most likely have crystals for self-love, relationships, protection and manifestation – they all have a unique space and role in your life, based on what you have learned about them. Thus, when you want to amplify a certain energy in your life, you likely know which crystal to reach for, and whether your decision is determined by color, shape, mineral content or pure intuition.

Aquamarine with schorl

My wish here is to complement the knowledge you have by sharing powerful new ways of working with crystals. In Part 3 of this book, I will be introducing you to crystals that connect to each of the seven chakras, some of which you may know and others that may be new to you, so that you can familiarize yourself with these and get to know their healing properties, too.

HOW CRYSTALS CHANNEL ENERGY

Just knowing your favorite crystal companion is nearby, or walking past your collection of crystals, can incite peace, joy and other positive emotions that raise the vibration of your own energy. The moment you interact with your crystals or hold them in your hands you are activated toward your intentions. Imagine reaching for a citrine crystal that you use for abundance meditations; the crystal reminds you of your plans for creating a bountiful stream of financial prosperity and sends you into a state of motivation to take action toward your goal. So, you bring your crystal with you into your office, set it down next to you and start working on the business you want to launch. Amplified by the citrine's golden presence and metaphysical properties, you gain confidence in your efforts, and become giddy and excited to receive the blessings that are ahead. Your crystal has your back!

Now, note the effects that this mental picture has on your body and energy supply — on your level of confidence and the quality of your mindset. Don't you want to jump up out of your seat and go achieve your goals right now? I sure do — and that's the transformative power of association, paired with stimulation of your physical senses. The capacity for these positive effects to continue growing bigger and more impactful in several different areas of your life is infinite, especially when you continuously work to maintain your highest vibration. This is when true change and manifestation begin to take shape in your world, and your visions become reality. To start the process, all you need to do is agree to commit to learning and to be willing to accept the support of your crystals in your transformation.

As tools for healing, crystals work on an energetic level, affecting our chakra system, which serves as the interface between our physical and subtle bodies.

THE CRYSTALS USED IN GEM SORCERY

In Part 3, you will discover that seven different crystals are assigned to each of the seven energy centers based on their healing properties. Each crystal is given an emphasized characteristic that upholds its portion in the overall balance of a fully functional chakra energy center (see page 31). All 49 crystals listed in the book can be utilized to amplify your meditations and direct energy flow throughout your body. Each crystal serves as a conduit and anchor for your intentions and illuminations (see page 83). Much like the new mental and emotional associations you will be making with your senses through the Gem Sorcery Method, your crystals will come to have new meanings attached to them, too. Through the meditations and tools in Part 3, you will be imbuing, or programming, your crystals with the information of your thoughts, aspirations, emotions and energy. This is foundational in reinforcing the healthy mindset shift of each chakra.

NOTE: There is no need to worry if you don't own every single crystal listed in this book. If you have just one for each chakra in Part 3, that single crystal will be enough for you to enjoy the meditations — and even if you currently have zero crystals, you can refer to the crystal imagery on those pages to receive the influential healing energy of crystals during the meditations. You will also see that there are crystal "substitutes" suggested for each of the chakras, so if you don't have one of the main seven chakra crystals, you can use one of these alternatives instead.

CREATE A GEM SORCERY JOURNAL

Action and repetition are the most productive ways to store new information in your memory, and develop your skills, so I would like you to get better acquainted with any crystals that you do have in your possession and to keep a note of your experiences with them in a journal. Hands-on sensory activation guided by intention and mindset will help you to begin your initiation into Gem Sorcery mind, body and spirit integration.

1. Take a moment to venture through your crystal collection, if you have one. Rub your fingers across their surfaces with your eyes closed. Feel their weight in your hands as you meditate on specific intentions and practice directing energy flow with them.

2. Place the crystals in purposeful areas of your space and experiment with your favorite pieces and rituals, based on what you learn in this book.

3. Use a journal to document what you found most useful about engaging with your crystals in this way, whether you feel more self-assured in your healing path, and what your level of energy and alignment are on a scale from 1 to 10, in comparison to before you started. Tune in to your mind, body and spirit and jot down everything that each aspect of your being is feeling in the moment.

Green apophyllite

THE SEVEN CHAKRAS

The Gem Sorcery Method works with the properties of crystals and meditations to heal the seven primary chakras — the energy centers in our body — and to keep these open and balanced so that life energy (*prana*) can flow freely through them for our optimum wellbeing. A symbiotic relationship exists between our mind, our body and our energy centers; by using crystals, meditations and other tools to channel intentional energy to our chakras, the correlating areas of our mind and body benefit also.

The seven chakras studied in this book can be visualized as a column running up the center of the body, from the root chakra at the base of the spine to the crown chakra floating directly at the top of your head. They are individually linked to endocrine glands that play essential roles in the chemical processes of the body. These glands secrete hormones that then impact physiological processes, such as reproduction, development, energy levels, breathing, sexuality and more. They achieve this by communicating with specific organs, tissues and cells of the body via the bloodstream. When viewing the body holistically — looking at all parts as a whole, synergistic system — it makes perfect sense that energy flow has a direct influence on its performance. Harmonizing your chakras, especially by means of conscious intention, energizes the related glands, thereby invigorating your bodily functions.

If one chakra is faulty, well, you can imagine the impact it will have on the chakras above it — the snowball effect of an imbalanced or blocked chakra should not be underestimated. When healing the chakras with the Gem Sorcery Method, treat each one as an individual leg of a large platform, that you and your wellness sit upon.

Without one leg,the rest are susceptible to weakness. When each leg is strong and well taken care of, the platform remains balanced and capable, thereby keeping you aligned and supported.

As you begin this journey, always remember to hold the vibration of the prior chakra in your mind and connect the flow of energy through each energy center. Keep in mind that everything is interconnected – once you work on one chakra, you must maintain its quality for the balancing of each subsequent energy center.

THE ORDER OF THE CHAKRAS

In addition to their interrelationships, the seven chakras energetically and vibrationally connect with specific colors and corresponding areas of the body, which we'll explore further in Part 3. You will discover many important characteristics, including the chakras' associated colors, their locations in the body, related physical senses and relevant sensory triggers (for the first five) and their endocrine glands as well as their spiritual, mental, emotional and physical manifestations of balance and imbalance. Examples of scenarios that can cause efficiency or deficiency are also provided.

Here is a list of the order in which we will be visiting them, starting with the root chakra at the base of the spine and working up to the crown:

- Root chakra (first energy center), red

- Sacral chakra (second energy center), orange

- Solar plexus chakra (third energy center), yellow

- Heart chakra (fourth energy center), green

- Throat chakra (fifth energy center), blue

- Third eye chakra (sixth energy center), indigo

- Crown chakra (seventh energy center), violet or white

Working from the bottom up, we will pay specialized attention to each energy center, awakening rising energy (*kundalini*) up the spinal column in the process. This energy, also known as life force or *prana*, is a key to the door of awareness.

You will discover how the colors of the chakras reflect the sequence of the rainbow and connect to crystals that share their hues and vibrations. As explained on page 37, colors link chakras and crystals to certain emotions and behaviors through the principles of color psychology and color therapy.

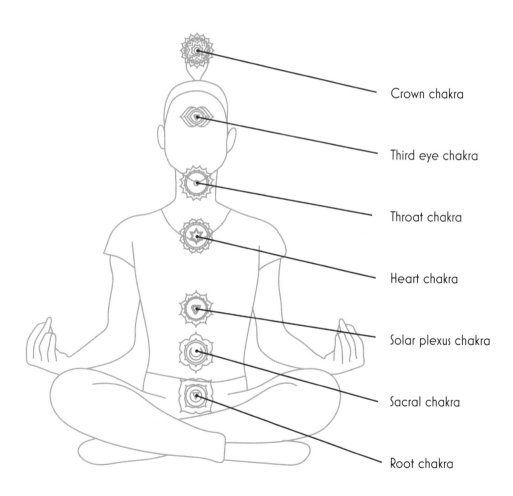

Crown chakra

Third eye chakra

Throat chakra

Heart chakra

Solar plexus chakra

Sacral chakra

Root chakra

CHAKRAS AND THE FIVE SENSES

Each of the first five primary chakras is linked to a physical sense such as smell (the root chakra) or sight (the solar plexus chakra). In my experience, the best way to become fully present in the body and make scattered, anxious thoughts coherent is by tuning into the senses – to become aware of what we taste, smell, touch, hear or see. From the moment we are born, these actions provide us with our understanding of the world, showing us what we like, what we don't like, what to pursue and what to move away from in order to maintain safety. These five senses are how we lift the veil of life's mysteries, come face to face with them and form our perspectives.

Most importantly, these five senses and the memories we create with them are often stored in our subconscious and unconscious minds, driving our behavior for a long time to come. Have you ever heard a song or smelled a scent that reminded you of the past? Whether the memory is positive or negative, you immediately recognize the sensation and your body responds as if you are reliving the experience all over again. Whatever other stories and thoughts you were thinking about in that moment become lost, even forgotten, after the sensory trigger. But what if we could use this phenomenon to our advantage by using the gift of sensually engaging with the world around us with intention and purpose – to generate sensations and store memories (or empowering mindsets) that make us better, happier people?

These first five chakras represent your childhood, and when activating the senses linked to them, you will be helping to release trauma from this part of your life. (If you find overwhelmingly painful memories surfacing, please seek support from a professional therapist or healthcare provider to help you process this if necessary.) It's worth noting that chakras can fall in and out of alignment at any time of life, but the most significant impact often happens during the developmental years and can be more difficult to address since the impacts are deeply embedded in the unconscious.

The third eye chakra (sixth energy center) is connected to pre-physical cognition and does not have a physical sense appointed to it. It pertains to conception and ancestral awareness – here is where you tap into your intuition, inner knowing and spirit to integrate subconscious ancestral shadows. The crown chakra (seventh energy center) also represents pre-physical awareness and pertains to the Universal Consciousness.

THE SUBTLE BODY

In addition to the physical body that we can see and touch, we have a subtle body that consists of seven layers of vibrating energy. Each layer vibrates at a slightly higher frequency as it moves farther away from the physical body. The layers of this body constitute the aura and can be captured with the aid of Kirlian photography, as well as perceived by the third eye. They are:

- Etheric body
- Emotional body
- Mental body
- Astral body
- Etheric template
- Celestial body
- Causal body

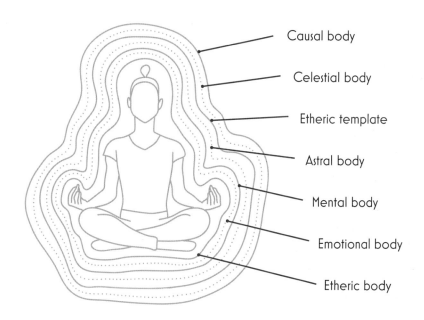

Causal body

Celestial body

Etheric template

Astral body

Mental body

Emotional body

Etheric body

Red hematite included quartz

Because the cells in your body create their own electromagnetic fields, their overall quality affects the magnitude of your aura, and your aura then sends information back into your body to direct physiological and chemical processes. The subtle and physical bodies are thus engaged in a continuous dance, influencing the quality of each other with their own health and vitality. With the proper inputs and rituals, this feedback loop between mind and body shifts from incoherent to coherent. The layers of your aura become stronger and more vibrant and, as a result, your mind and body become healthier and more resilient.

You will find the correspondences of each of these layers of the subtle body and the chakras listed in Part 3. The chakras act as anchors for the layers, and by balancing the chakras you will help to strengthen the connections between these different layers of your existence for your optimum wellbeing.

CHAKRAS AND THE NATURAL WORLD

In addition to our personal connection, the seven chakras also hold correspondences with the natural world. These range all the way from plants to specific locations. Certain environments strongly resonate with the energetic qualities of specific chakras, providing an opportunity to deepen your connection with these energy centers. I've detailed the evocative environments for each chakra in Part 3 and provided further insights into these connections in Bringing Gem Sorcery into the World on pages 240–3.

Another exciting aspect of the Gem Sorcery Method relates to the mystical world of plant medicine. You will have a chance to explore herbs and/or essential oils that correspond with the essences of the root and sacral chakras, and engage your senses of smell and taste, respectively. Of course, there are other options for the sensory activation of these energy centers besides herbs, such as flowers (for smell) and food (for taste) – but dabbling in a bit of herbalism is always a fun learning opportunity!

COLOR
CONNECTIONS

Color is not only a feast for the eyes but a gift for the human mind and body. When we perceive colors, what we're essentially seeing is energy and vibration, making color the perfect tool for balancing the vibrations of the chakras and for use through the medium of crystals.

Each color in the spectrum is believed to possess a unique energy and vibration that can affect the body in particular ways and be used to treat a range of physical and emotional conditions. For example, red is thought to stimulate the circulatory system and increase energy levels, while blue is believed to promote relaxation and reduce stress. According to the principles of color psychology, colors can subtly influence our moods and perceptions, too – from stirring our passions, to linking us to the Divine.

Color therapy, also known as chromotherapy, is an alternative healing modailty that utilizes the energy and psychological effects of colors to restore balance and promote healing in the mind, body and spirit. The practice of color therapy dates back to ancient times, with evidence of its use in Egypt, China and India. And when it comes to harnessing the power of color therapy, crystals are one of the most abundant sources available. For example, a red crystal may be used to support the healing of the root chakra, which governs the body's physical needs and survival instincts. Similarly, a blue crystal may be used to support the throat chakra, which governs communication and self-expression.

Color therapy doesn't have to be complicated or time-consuming. In fact, you can engage in this alternative form of healing with simple actions like wearing a specific color to match or enhance your moods. Feeling down and blue? Why not slip into something yellow to bring a ray of sunshine into your day? You can also incorporate color therapy into your home decor by strategically placing items of a particular color to balance certain emotions. As an example, if you're feeling sluggish, a pop of red can help stimulate your energy levels. With a touch of creativity, you can explore numerous ways to incorporate color into your daily life, allowing you to channel the chakra energy you wish to embrace.

Nature is the most magnificent source for color therapy. Simply take a stroll outside and absorb the various colors of the earth, from the green of the trees to the blue of the sky, to help restore balance and promote healing. Another easy way to engage in color therapy is by replacing standard white light bulbs with colored light bulbs instead. Various hues of light can influence your mood and vitality differently, so explore different colors to discover what suits you best. Warm, yellow-toned light can promote relaxation, while cool, blue-toned light can enhance focus and productivity. Whether you choose to wear vibrant attire or adorn your living space with a spectrum of colors, integrating color therapy into your daily routine can profoundly enhance your overall wellbeing.

In the Gem Sorcery Method, we utilize the knowledge that humans are naturally drawn to colors – they are critical to our existence and evoke emotions, memories and sensations from the time we are babies, all the way up until the end of our lives. We tap into the power of color psychology and color therapy to increase the effectiveness of crystals and their properties, strengthening our associations with them and magnifying their healing influence on the chakras. When working with the restorative nature of color therapy with my clients, I take what I learn about my clients' lifestyles and energetics and establish environmental recommendations for their healing practices. In the case of individual chakras, I look at client history, experiences and the overall balance of the energy center (whether overactive or underactive) to determine how to use color to create greater harmony in their lives. In Part 3, I've provided color psychology correspondences for all seven chakras to assist you in selecting crystals for balancing each energy center.

Citrine

SHADOW WORK

Throughout this book, you will notice I talk about the "shadow." This refers to the shadow self, or shadow mindset, which represents the subconscious and unconscious minds, and the behaviors that they influence without our cognizance. As I mentioned before, these behaviors are often motivated by energetic, ancestral genetics and/or repressed memories, most commonly from childhood.

The most transformative and life-changing step I took on my healing journey was delving into the depths of my shadow self. I uncovered that each unresolved traumatic experience in my life had fragmented a piece of my spirit, creating energy leaks as these fragments wandered aimlessly within my auric field. These imbalances eventually manifested in my physical body, leaving me susceptible to a range of issues. By illuminating my own shadow, I began to witness the myriad ways I lived through the lens of my programs. I was able to pinpoint how my traumas manifested in the spiritual, mental, emotional and physical aspects of my being, and how these are intricately linked together.

It became evident that we all run repetitive programs and patterns rooted in past experiences, leading to the recurrence of familiar stories and outcomes that constrain our potential. Approximately 95 percent of who we are as individuals is dominated by the subconscious memories we carry around; our daily actions are frequently driven by these hidden aspects of self. These patterns persist within our DNA and can be epigenetically inherited by future generations until we consciously recognize and transform these programs into something more constructive and empowering. (Epigenetics is the study of how our behaviors and environment can affect the way our genes express themselves. However, unlike genetic changes, epigenetic changes are reversible and do not change our DNA sequence, although they may change how our body reads a DNA sequence.) Essentially, we have the ability to turn "on" or "off" the genes passed down through our bloodline, by taking mindful action and engaging in preventative care. Therefore, it's crucial to identify and reclaim all the aspects of ourselves that we might have overlooked or neglected after significant life events. By reintegrating these parts into our physical and subtle bodies, we achieve a more complete and balanced existence – not only for ourselves, but also for the sake of our own children.

In my case, my emotional reaction to my poor physical health negatively impacted my mental health and left me spiritually empty. That spiritual void then perpetuated more dark emotions, and, in turn, I made disempowering decisions that continued to destroy my physical health. I existed in a feedback loop that persistently confirmed my identity as a "sick person."

Notice how this situation can quickly become complicated. One issue can trigger another, and you may find yourself unconsciously reacting based on past wounds or stories that deeply affect your life. Alternatively, you can choose to make these wounds conscious, embark on a healing process, and regain control of your inherent power. I chose to do the latter and my hope is that, after reading this book, you will know how to regain your power and heal, too.

REPROGRAMMING USING THE SENSES

Integrating the fragmented parts of yourself is a fundamental aspect of self-discovery and healing in adulthood. Without focusing on each aspect of ourselves through our senses, the roots of our issues will maintain their stronghold, forming a cycle of dysfunction and making it difficult for us to leave destructive behaviors in the past.

Activating the senses with intention through the power of association is a potent method for drawing energy inward, sealing leaks in the auric field, replacing disruptive patterns with healing actions and promoting positive stimulation of the brain, emotions and the body's physiological processes.

By consistently practicing the mindful sensory meditations and exercises that I share in Part 3, the relationship I had with the wisdom of my body changed. It spoke to me more clearly than ever before, providing me with valuable insight as to where I held repressed energy, what symptoms of disease were beginning to manifest as a result, what caused the blockage in the first place, and how to move through it to heal it. This shift from unconscious patterns to conscious awareness is what I call "illumination" – the antidote to the subconscious effects of the "shadow" that I spoke of earlier. By identifying the "shadow" of the subconscious mind and replacing it with a conscious "illumination," we intentionally write a new program into the hardware of the brain, thereby deconstructing and disempowering old neural connections to accommodate new, constructive connections.

The fusion of the mind's power, the wisdom of both the physical and energetic bodies, and the clarity and awareness facilitated by crystal medicine creates the essence of the illumination mindset. All come together to guide you toward your favorite version of self, much like the varying wavelengths of light in a flashlight guide you to your next destination in the dark. By harmonizing my spiritual, mental, emotional and physical wellbeing, I assumed control and creative agency over my reality.

STEPPING INTO YOUR TRUE SELF

Bringing back the lost aspects of ourselves and awakening the subconscious can be unsettling as it confronts our long-held beliefs about who we are. Each identity that shaped our sense of self becomes a distinct entity, stripped away and observable from an objective standpoint. Frequently, during this process, we may come to realize that the identity in question was not our authentic nature, but rather a product of our conditioning or an inheritance from our ancestors' experiences through epigenetics.

Yet without these identities, we are left in vulnerable, uncharted territory: "If I was never actually this person, then who am I?" This open-ended unknown can be scary, or it can be exciting. This is the fork in the road that determines whether we go back to our usual programming, or create a new reality for ourselves – one that is based on who we were before everyone told us who we "should" be. Initially, reshaping the narratives that shape our identity and evolving into more authentic versions of ourselves might appear complex. However, all we truly require are awareness and a willingness to begin.

PART 2

HOW TO WORK WITH GEM SORCERY

SETTING INTENTIONS

Before explaining the process of programming crystals, it's beneficial to establish some context for this practice. Its effectiveness hinges on our mindset, inner alignment and our overarching intention to transition from shadow to illumination. As adults, we have the ability to process information consciously and assign the meanings we choose to the stimuli we receive. Taking that capability and alchemizing it with innocent, child-like wonder via our senses is a superpower. And this is partly what I mean by intention here.

Through deliberately connecting with your Inner Child – the part of your subconscious that began picking up messages from your environment before it was fully able to process them mentally and emotionally – and rediscovering your wonder for the world by engaging your senses, you are setting the intention to move from shadow to illumination with a focus tempered by playfulness. There is a reason that creativity is linked to the Inner Child: children are inherently more receptive and conscious of their surroundings, while also maintaining a joyful perspective of the world around them. Most children do not have to endure the same stresses many adults do; they see the beauty of life through untainted eyes. But what happens when they do endure the heavy weight of traumas that are too difficult even for adults to bear? They can lose trust and close themselves off from others, and the resulting dissonance can have significant consequences in the years to come. As part of our healing process, we will be inviting that lost Inner Child to come out and play again.

During my own healing journey, I worked intimately and deliberately with my Inner Child. She reminded me of the absolute magic in every unique moment. I trusted her to be safe and free in her

Celestite

innocence, and engage her senses as she moved through the world. Setting this trust in motion gave me the confidence to truly love myself without judgment and find gratitude in everything I was going through. There she was, my sweet Inner Child, showing me that I was meant to attain powerful wisdom by way of my pain, and that I would find it by opening my heart and surrendering to the eternal present. I began to focus on visualizing and developing the reality I wanted to live. Through this shift in focus, my thoughts became a match for the frequency of my goals.

Quickly, my body began responding to my reconstructed mindset and self-talk with higher energy levels, greater mental clarity, more confidence, reduced anxiety and a positive outlook on life that confirmed I was on the right path. I realized that, if I could hack my mental and emotional health and witness such radical transformation in my physiology as a result, I could take it a step further by mastering my physical body — learning its cues, developing a strong understanding of how it functions and making it stronger through exercise and proper nutrition. Naturally, my spirituality was revitalized and my heart started to beat with the energy of the Collective Consciousness. I felt the intrinsic web of universal connectedness flowing through my mind, body and spirit. I sought out ways to further amplify my relationship with spirit, thereby leading to my studies in vibrational energy medicine and crystal healing. I was on my way . . .

INTENTION AND ALIGNMENT

The mind, body and spirit support one another to co-create a fully optimized and functional existence. When all are healthy and in alignment, communication between each aspect is amplified and uplifted. Stagnation is diminished, if not eradicated, and energy moves more freely throughout the body.

When energy moves more freely, the body is better able to correspond efficiently with the brain by sending and receiving signals for taking action. These signals then influence the chemical processes that occur within the body, which impact the quality of life and health of the individual that it belongs to. If energy is blocked, and the body or brain are sickly, it is possible that the mind will be more prone to darkness, and vice versa; however, because the mind is made up of human consciousness, it can be changed by choice — and when the mind is changed in a beneficial way, with intention, the opportunity for healing becomes stronger.

The thoughts, perspectives and beliefs that the mind holds on to play a significant role in the types of messages that the brain and body receive, thereby making a supportive and positive mindset a critical factor in the mind–body connection. If the mindset is centered on negative outcomes, such as illness or death, we may witness the evolution of illness within the body, perfectly illustrating the self-fulfilling prophecy. Such expectations can become subconscious authority figures that influence our actions, behaviors and emotions that, ultimately, alter our neural pathways and determine the fate of our physical body. We witness miracles, however, when people choose to continue living fully and mindfully, with the intention of making progress, mentally, spiritually, emotionally and physically.

In its healthiest state, the physical body is a welcoming vehicle to the spirit that resides within it. The individual spirit becomes tangible when it converges with the mind's awareness of physical existence. Before this, it is omnipresent as universal energy. Through its marriage with the consciousness of the human mind, the spirit is capable of perceiving its purpose, and interacting as an individual with the world around it, including with the physical body that provides it with sacred space. The spirit energy is naturally one with the Collective Consciousness, or superconscious, and the physical serves as a mirror to reflect it back to itself.

The brain and physical body must be unified with both spirit and mind consciousness in order to be considered alive. Without the mind, the body would not have conscious direction for the chemical and electrical processes that are the catalyst for its proper functioning; the mind makes our daily choices, such as what food to consume, what exercise to partake in and how much sunlight to absorb through the skin, etc.

The Spirit, on the other hand, gives the body and mind access to what I call "pings from Source" (the Source being a term for the Universal Consciousness that connects us all) in the form of flashes of intuition and "gut instincts." In other words, intuition is a messenger that disperses the wisdom of the superconscious, where it is then felt as a physical sensation, most often within the chest or gut, and received by the consciousness of the mind to be interpreted. The mind's perception then influences the brain and body to respond as necessary.

If the mind is healthy, so too will be the messaging, establishing a pathway that allows us to develop an *appropriate* response in relation to the situation. However, if the mind is unhealthy, the filter through which thought is directed may trigger a downward mental spiral and activate the sympathetic nervous system, thereby sending the body into a state of fight or flight, even when the situation does not require such an extreme response. It is essential to mention that, because the subconscious mind is so frequently in charge of our thoughts and behaviors, it will run the reaction in the direction of its existing programming. If that programming consists of fear, pessimism or any other number of low-frequency emotions due to our carrying repressed memories and traumas, our subconscious must first be sent into a higher frequency state through awareness and reprogramming techniques. This work makes the difference between the mind as a prison, or the mind as a key to freedom.

Knowing all of this, it is crucial to ask ourselves whether a spirit can truly be free and in its most attuned state, while housed in a physical body that isn't properly functioning. Likewise, can a physical body and brain overflow with abundant health and activation, when paired with a disconnected spirit and negative mind? When you imagine that the nutrition you consume to fuel your physical body, as well as the media you entertain yourself with, for example, either enlivens your spirit, or diminishes it, would you choose to respect your body and select your fuel wisely? The answer is most likely yes; however, many people intentionally choose this path only when they fully grasp the delicate interconnectedness of mind, body and spirit.

At this stage of recognition and understanding, people are initiated into their personal power and start taking action that is in alignment with their intention to embody their Higher Self. Take note of this statement, because *action being in alignment with intention* is the main element in achieving success in any goal or practice, especially when working with crystals and meditations to rebalance the chakras in Gem Sorcery.

Rose quartz sphere

PROGRAMMING CRYSTALS

Programming your crystals, or setting your intentions for them, is a straightforward practice for prescribing personalized associations to their energies. The purpose of setting an intention is to materialize your mind's vibrational frequency into the physical. You can do this by either saying it out loud, writing it down or preferably both. For example, you might choose to set your intention to vibrate at a frequency that attracts high-quality, aligned relationships into your life that make you a better person in mind, body and spirit. In this instance, you could write down, or speak out

Smokey quartz

loud, a sentence that goes something like: "I imbue this crystal with the energy and intention of raising my vibration up to my full potential, thereby attracting high-quality relationships that are direct reflections of the elevated path I am choosing to walk today — we will make each other stronger, better and more purposeful every day, making life more magical and aligned with my vision."

Words themselves carry unique vibrations that have the capability to shift the frequency of all that they make contact with. Be sure that the words you choose to speak are in alignment with who you are being and how you intend to impact the world. Words are powerful initiators that, especially when supported with the equivalent actions, bring into existence the physical form of what was once just a simple thought.

ENERGY HYGIENE

Maintaining a frequency that is an energetic match for what you are calling in through your intentions is made easier, and more efficient, by practicing crystal programming. You are a human with complex emotions, so your bioenergetic field will be affected by not only your thoughts, but also the outside energy you come into contact with. This includes energy from other people, food, music and manmade electromagnetic fields (also known as non-native EMF), to name a few. A crystal that is imbued with your highest intentions serves as your electromagnetic reminder to elevate yourself back into a state of alignment.

As you master raising your energy, it will become easier to maintain a heightened frequency in the presence of lower vibrations. Over time, you will start choosing what you allow to affect your energy in the first place, as well as what you surround yourself with that has the potential to change how you feel. Once you know it's possible to reclaim your personal power, there truly is no looking back, or accepting the things that bring you down – and this is the ultimate objective of the Gem Sorcery Method.

I call this crystal practice "energy hygiene." Energy hygiene is as valuable as physical hygiene, yet it is highly underestimated in its ability to solve challenges, whether mental, emotional, spiritual or physical. When you feel low, one of the best things you can do for yourself is shower in the radiance of a crystal, which holds and reflects your greatest visions and purpose. Make a daily, or even hourly, ritual of resetting your personal energy with a programmed crystal to continue magnetizing the outcome of your dreams. Carry small crystals with you to work, school or on your travels, and reactivate your energy at any moment throughout your day.

Baby steps like these add up over time to form habits that increase the resonance of your bioenergetic field. When you start, it may become as valuable a daily ritual as your morning cup of coffee. In fact, it is very likely that you may have been using your crystals in this way all along, carrying them with you everywhere you go and setting them on your desk at work – sensing that they are helpful, but perhaps not knowing how they are helping. However, through the Gem Sorcery Method, you will gain a working knowledge of the how and why, so you can be even more intentional about applying crystal healing energy to your life with focused clarity and direction.

CRYSTAL SHAPES

Crystals come in many different shapes and sizes. Some are cut and polished to give them particular shapes, while others maintain their natural earth-given configuration. Each type of crystal shape acts as a catalyst for tapping into a certain kind of energy, and affects the way it feels to make contact with it, which then determines how it is utilized in healing practices and rituals.

Certain shapes are perceived to direct energy flow in particular ways. For example, terminated crystals generally either direct or transmute energy, while spheres send energy out in all directions due to their symmetrical and rounded nature. Pyramids are exceptional for amplifying and focusing energy from the root to crown chakra, and so on so forth. The way in which different crystal shapes direct energy is particularly useful to understand when meditating, when placing crystals around your home or space and when cultivating more precise vibrations that are in harmony with your goals. While the raw material of the crystal itself always takes precedence, shapes offer an opportunity to take your Gem Sorcery practice to the next level.

Although there are an abundance of crystal shapes to work with, here I will be covering the most well-known and widely used crystal shapes, including how they can be put to use in rituals, meditations, contact therapy (how to handle them), harmonizing your environment and directing energy.

RAW

Raw crystals and minerals retain the original shapes and textures they were formed in while in the earth. They are not cut or polished by humans, and come in a variety of materials and formations. Some form as single terminations, some as clusters with many terminations, chunks and boulders, geodes and more. Their textures

can be smooth, rough, bubbly, glassy — even flaky, depending on the mineral. Many people celebrate crystals in their raw form for their natural beauty and earthy essence, and claim they have stronger energy because they have not been shape-shifted by the hands and consciousness of an individual human. Rather, raw crystals and minerals harness the consciousness of the earth.

Working with raw crystals and minerals in rituals and meditations invites us to take an in-depth look at who we truly are in our rawest form — without the conditioning and programming we pick up from the world and people around us. I like to call raw crystals "remembering crystals," because they serve as

Raw himalayan quartz

reminders of our creation and conception. They bring us back to the magic of our development in the womb, and the vibrant future of possibilities granted to us as we continue to grow. Raw crystals magnify our DNA when meditating with them to access our genetic material and consciously analyze where, and how, it was impacted by our environment, behaviors and ancestral wounds. In this state, we are better able to clear the slate of our learned limiting beliefs and behaviors, and start anew on the path to our embodied Higher Self.

INTENTION

While utilizing raw crystals and minerals in your practices, set the intention of learning about every corner of yourself and your existence, as these crystals were at the first union of physical body with spirit consciousness. This will lead to meaningful self-discovery that will change the course of your healing, and comfortability in your authenticity, for a long time to come.

CONTACT THERAPY

With raw crystals, especially during meditation, create a physical connection with them by holding them in your hands or setting them on a surface within close reach. You will notice that raw crystals offer a vast ocean of sensory stimulation to discover. Because they are completely natural, they may have sharp edges, points, lines and uneven markings on their surfaces. Close your eyes and gently draw your fingers over every edge, point and surface. Visualize the portion of the crystal you are making contact with and notice the similarities you and the crystal have – complex and unique, yet stable and strong. Both you and the crystal are composed of natural codes that created your final form, and carry an inspiring story from conception to present moment. Journey through your codes, remember your story and clear your energy.

ENVIRONMENT

Harmonize your environment and direct energy with raw crystals or minerals by placing one in each corner of the room(s) where you do your deepest reflection. Visualize the crystals in each corner as anchors to remind you of your truest self. The corners are symbolic of the nooks and crannies that exist within you, which make you who you are. When your crystals are in place, the room may feel more grounded, stable and organized. Energy will flow from corner to corner, and hold you in a state of centered awareness as you deep dive into your being. Each crystal communicates with the other and their energies meet you in the center of the room, like the midpoint of an X. Imagine the feeling of being safely held, wrapped up and suspended in a hammock – this is the feeling you will have when sitting, or standing, in the center of a room with raw crystals placed in each corner.

SPHERE

Spheres are shaped on a three-headed machine. They first begin as large chunks of raw stone that are ground down to a much smaller size, before being polished into a perfectly round and symmetrical shape. Spheres come in giant, large, medium, small and even miniature sizes. Although some raw crystals naturally come in a rounded shape, those are considered to be botryoidal, and are not perfectly symmetrical like a polished sphere. Most of the time, the surface of a mineral sphere is completely smooth, depending on the material. For example, pyrite can be shaped into a sphere, and most frequently expresses chunky sections of raw crystallization. Malachite is another example of a sphere that can be fully polished, but commonly comes with raw, velvety surfaces that are left untouched by the lapidary artist who performed the shaping and polishing process.

As the 3D versions of a circle, crystal spheres are symbolic of totality, completeness and oneness. For this reason, spheres are beneficial in rituals and meditations for connecting to Universal Consciousness, and Source energy – the space of knowing that you are all and all is you, and all creation in the Universe is Source-consciousness, experiencing itself as a reflection. In profound, meditative moments of conscious unity with Source, in which the ego no longer distinguishes itself as a separate entity, you gain access to the messages and guidance of Spirit. You become part of the Whole – where perception is experience, rather than judgment. Here, you unlock the door to mind, body and spirit integration and walk in fearless embodiment of your inner knowing – boundless and free, as is perfectly mirrored in the shape of a sphere. There are no sharp edges, or twists and turns. All there is, is infinity.

INTENTION

Prior to working with crystal spheres in your practice, set your intentions for releasing aspects of your ego that may be keeping you stuck in the cyclical process of entertaining that which no longer serves you. Prepare to clear attachment to the trappings of your struggles and recognize you are deserving of a harmonious, fruitful existence – not despite your experiences, but because of them. In doing so, you exist in a state of trust and resonance with Source, which makes you an energetic match for all things in alignment with your highest purpose.

Blue lace agate sphere

CONTACT THERAPY

This is most potent when two spheres of equal sizes are placed, one in each hand, during meditation. The density of the round shape in the middle of the palm serves as a mechanism for centering your consciousness. Then, from a place of still awareness, you can tap into the energy swirling around the room — how it reaches the surface of the sphere, absorbs into its core and immediately radiates outward again to fill the space. This process occurs over and over again, and all energies, including your own, are synchronized in a dance of unity and solidarity — all muses of Source. Gently roll the spheres in your hands, then close your fingers into a fist to squeeze the crystal and transfer your intention directly into it. Open your fingers and release the intention out into the room, to be assimilated into the Universe. You and your intentions are one with all.

ENVIRONMENT

Placing a sphere in the center of a room amplifies your environment by absorbing and reflecting all energy it comes into contact with. The sphere acts like a spearhead and transmits the overall vibration of the space. Thus, it is appropriate to set one at the center of a coffee table, or in the middle of the mantle above your fireplace, for example. For the same reason, they make excellent centerpieces in crystal grids designed for magnifying specific goals and intentions. When designing a space, such as an office, bedroom or living room, it is helpful to first establish the vibe you want the room to emanate. Based on that, conscientiously select a sphere made with the mineral that is the closest match to the atmosphere you intend to create. Color, size and mineral type are all relevant to your decision. If you want a room to exude romance, you could select rose quartz or rhodochrosite. For protection in the work place, choose something like black tourmaline or obsidian. Walking into a room with a sphere as a focal point thoroughly shifts how it feels and anyone who comes into contact with it will experience the formidable nature of your manifestations.

PALM STONE

Palm stones are cut and polished into an oval shape that is domed on both sides. They are smooth and perfectly sized to fit in (you guessed it) the palm of your hand. Depending on the material, palm stones can be dense, lightweight or in between. They are available in a variety of sizes to provide you with options based on what feels best to hold in your hands, or on your body. The size and weight are important to consider, because palm stones are intended to function as grounding stones, and are commonly used in healing practices to extract worry, stress and anxiety from the body. A variety of small palm stones, commonly known as "worry stones" (I prefer to call them "recalibration stones"), have an indentation on the back that is purposefully designed for you to rub your thumb over to reduce tension and enhance mindfulness. The same concept applies with palm stones, but due to their more proportionally rounded form, they have a more stabilizing effect that brings your body directly into alignment with the earth.

The word "oval" comes from the Latin *ovum*, which you likely already know means "egg." Formed in the image of an oval, palm stones connect the mind and body to the spirit of fertility and strength, as well as the immovable resilience of the Divine Feminine. By virtue of their very nature, palm stones are ideal for channeling the sacred energy of Mother Earth — the most incredible force to be reckoned with. Mother Earth is grounded, steadfast (even when she shakes), enduring and produces transformational intensity that is felt far and wide. Like the roots of a tree, harnessing this penetrating energy grounds you in your flesh and establishes a reliable, secure base for you to reach for the heights of your purpose and intuition. When you quiver from self-doubt or fear, meditating with a palm stone reminds you of your capable, roaring spirit and to continue growing, and thriving, above and beyond your comfort zone. You are secure to your core and confident in your abilities. The Divine Feminine stretches and expands, birthing awareness and inner knowing in those with the intention to awaken to it within themselves.

Ocean jasper palm stone

INTENTION

Set your intention on merging your spirit with your physical body when working
with palm stones, and generate a plan of action for retrieving your greatest visions
and birthing them into reality. Seek clarity from your intuition, guided by the Divine
Feminine. Nourish the counsel you receive by planting hardy seeds of purpose in the
soil of your creativity. By doing so, they will grow deeply rooted into the earth, and
cultivate a life true to your happiest, freest, most courageous and authentic expression.

CONTACT THERAPY

Hold two palm stones in the center of your palms (one in each hand), which are metaphysically in alignment with your intention and purpose, to connect with this crystal shape. The stones will create a weighted sensation in your hands and arms, promoting a deepening of bodily awareness and security within your existence. Set the back of your hands on the ground, with the palm stones still in your palms, and drop your shoulders down to ease into a nurturing stillness. Roll the stones around in your hands and take note of the connection your skin makes with the smooth surface to activate your Divine Feminine consciousness. The rounded dome on top of the stones receives energy from your spirit and intuition, and gently wraps the stone with your intention. The bottom dome, which is in contact with your palm, sends the intention downward — to be established in the physical realm. You may also place the palm stones on specific points of your body to accomplish the same goal, always focusing on the connection your skin makes with the stone. Here, your mind, body and spirit integrate, to transmit messages between each other that support your greatest visions.

ENVIRONMENT

Plant reminders of your goals and intentions in your immediate environment by selecting places to which you frequently pay attention, and placing palm stones that you associate with your intentions in those locations. For example, there may be a table where you put your car keys every day — place a palm stone on it as a reminder to spur you into taking action toward accomplishing your ambitions. These crystal reminders serve as "accountability buddies," which hold you to your commitment to bring your visions into physical existence. Having these reminder crystals around you affords you the opportunity to pick them up and hold them in your palms for a moment of grounding and centering meditation. This is a simple act that has the potential to impact your mindset and energy levels positively for the rest of the day, leaving you calm, motivated and focused.

PYRAMID

The crystal pyramid is a polished powerhouse with four triangular faces that rise up from a flat, square base to form an apex. It is a shape that has charmed and hypnotized the world since ancient times. Crystal pyramids are the epitome of the beauty that arises from the collaboration between the earth and our human consciousness. A variety of sizes are available in this shape; however, the largest of these is comparatively small when compared to other crystal shapes and, to my knowledge, there are no giant crystal pyramids in existence, as there are spheres and towers. No matter the size of the pyramid, however, the energy of this shape is formidable and penetrating in its presence; therefore, a crystal pyramid of any size is a valuable addition to your crystal collection. You can find them in almost every mineral and color, making them instrumental tools for a variety of different healing intentions.

Made up primarily of triangles, pyramids represent enlightenment and manifestation, and the existence of a Higher Self. They symbolize strength, balance and integration of the mind, body and spirit — symbolized by the three sides that make up a triangle. The power of three is frequently referenced in culture and religion, often suggesting a wholeness that is achieved when three subjects, or energies, converge.

The square-shaped pyramid base signifies stability and the physical earth. "Earth, air, water, fire" and "north, south, east, west" are two excellent examples of the way the number four influences and directs our lives on the physical plane.

Through the unification of these two meaningful numerological symbols, the pyramid becomes the model crystal shape for rituals and meditations to amplify the mind-body-spirit connection (and are particularly productive after successfully centering your energy in the core of your physical body by using palm stone energy), thus enabling the impactful manifestation of your ideal reality.

INTENTION

Before working with pyramids, set your intention on speaking with your mind, body and spirit as though they are separate entities, which you have the fortune of learning about intimately and intrinsically. Pay attention to what each one says to you about what is needed, as well as what is already flowing abundantly in the direction of its utmost health. In doing so, you will gain understanding of what work must be done, and what type of plan should be put in place to construct a more expansive foundation for holding up the amplified version of your brightest Highest Self.

Angelite pyramid

CONTACT THERAPY

Wherever you choose to place a pyramid during contact therapy, on your body or in your hands, envision a clear materialization of your desired physical reality. On a piece of paper, describe this vision in detail and place the paper under the pyramid; visualize the reality being held and supported by its stable base. From there, in your thoughts, send the vision up through the apex of the pyramid to be magnified by the Universe. (When, with practice, you are able to hold the vision with clarity in your mind, you may choose to skip writing it down and simply imagine yourself opening one of the triangle faces of the pyramid like a door, and placing your mind's image on the base inside.) The contact that the base of the pyramid makes with your body relates to the stability and anchoring of your own physical being. Then, like an electrified cyclone, your manifestations swirl upward and are projected into the ether to be heard. You may also receive energy and guidance through the apex, drawn downward into the base for your body to distribute. When working with the pyramid in this way, it is beneficial to place it on the specific chakra you are seeking to balance and/or activate.

ENVIRONMENT

Because pyramids are so energizing, they are best reserved for spaces in which you seek to be invigorated. Harmonious environments for crystal pyramids might include your workspace, a room where you frequently gather with family and friends, or your exercise space. If you seek to utilize a pyramid for romantic purposes, you may choose to work with it in your bedroom, even if this is normally your quiet zone. Ultimately, your intention is the most vital determining factor in where you choose to place your pyramid, and if amplification is what you strive for in that space, then I encourage you to experiment with the location. Pyramids make for great centerpieces at dinner tables, or at meetings where you wish to share your deepest, most valuable thoughts with other likeminded people. Your spoken manifestations and ideas will reverberate through the Universe, and pick up momentum to be actualized in the physical realm.

GENERATOR

Generator crystals are polished towers that are characterized by six identical triangular faces meeting at the point of termination. The six faces make this shape a "generator" rather than a "tower." Much like a tower, however, generators have a flat base that enables them to stand on their own, making them magical display pieces and centerpieces for crystal grids and meditations. Although this variety of termination can be found in nature, those are extremely rare and the majority of these crystals are polished, so be aware of this fact if adopting a generator crystal into your collection.

Generators are available in many minerals, colors and sizes. Because of this diversity, they can be utilized in a wide range of practices aimed at bringing forth any intention you choose. Whether you wish to amplify the energies of love and romance, wealth and abundance, peace and tranquility, or focus and clarity, crystal generators are special companions to have by your side for all of your manifestation purposes!

In rituals and meditations assisted by crystal generators, it is important to take note of the spiritual significance of the number six and weave that wisdom into your intentions, before beginning your practice. The number six is symbolic of the "sixth sense," which I consider to be intuition and seeing with the third eye. It is not a tangible sense, like the other five, but it can be clearly felt and observed by the individual experiencing it.

Keeping in mind the intuition and clairvoyance that arise in alignment with the use of crystal generators, initiate your personal sixth sense to receive guidance from your Higher Self before any meditation with them. The direction coming from your Higher Self always intends to serve you and your highest good – intuition is designed to lead you toward the path of your most favorable outcome. Ask your Higher Self, "What is the best next step in reaching my intended goal or purpose?" Once you receive a clear response, paint a detailed picture in your mind of what taking that step looks and feels like. Go as far as playing out all the positive impacts that taking the step will have on all the different areas of your life. Feel it as though you are already experiencing it to prime your vibration for calling in blessings. True to its name, the generator crystal *generates* a frequency that matches your own and projects it, through its six triangle faces, into the Universe for amplification.

INTENTION

Prior to collaborating with a generator crystal, set the intention of paving a clear channel of transmission between your intuition and conscious mind. Remove any doubts you may have regarding your capability to hear your intuition speak. Recognize that you do not need to pressure your Higher Self to speak with you — it is a built in-mechanism you were gifted with the moment you became a conscious being. By understanding this, you will build confidence in your ability to hear it.

CONTACT THERAPY

The greatest benefit of physically connecting your body with a generator crystal is the remarkable energy exchange that occurs — a continuous flow of your conscious thought passes through your body and delivers itself to be held within the crystal. For this reason, generators are excellent conduits for precisely channeling intention and vital life force in whichever direction you want it to go. Use your generator as a wand by wrapping your dominant hand around its base. Then rub your thumb along the body of the crystal and engage with the warming friction it produces. As you do this, your brain will be activated by its analysis of the smooth surface, the edges of the facets and the gradually increasing warmth of the generator crystal under your finger. Associate your brain's perceptions of this sensation of touch with the magnification of your manifestation abilities. Imagine them building up and gaining strength — rising up like a tidal wave, pouring vitality into your intentions and emboldening your mindset. Open the channel between the generator point and your hand to receive the insight of your intuition. Through this practice, you will program your mind to associate holding the generator with bringing forth your utmost confidence and supercharging your ability to embody your Higher Self and live your highest purpose.

ENVIRONMENT

Precisely like your mind, body and spirit, your environment benefits greatly from synchronizing with generator crystal energy. Spaces that assimilate well with this shape include meditation rooms, altars, art rooms and work places. Anywhere you ideate, visualize, create and manifest will benefit from the presence of a generator crystal. Consider the gravity and potential of your visions, then enhance your chosen environment with a generator crystal that is adequate in size for holding and transmitting your manifestations, as well as receiving the messages of your intuition. The larger and bolder your dreams, the better! Set the generator directly in front of you as the centerpiece on your desk, workbench or altar space. Ensure that it is effortlessly within reach so you can make contact with it at any moment; placing your hands on the generator should become a habit that not only reinforces your association to a more empowered mindset, but opens the flow of transmission and reception between you and your sixth sense.

Lepidolite generator

SKULL

Crystal skulls are hand carved, detailed replicas of the human skull, usually crafted by artisan stoneworkers. The intention placed by the lapidarist into skull carvings can often be perceived the moment you pick these crystals up. While there are many people who are loyal to raw crystal energy over all other types, crystal skull enthusiasts contend that these shapes are unparalleled in the spiritual impact they are capable of inspiring within those who work with them. Skulls are spiritually versatile, too, owing to the fact that they are carved from a large selection of minerals — there are no limitations to the colors, energies and sizes available with which to cultivate the manifestation of a multitude of intentions.

When you gaze at this crystal shape, essentially you are viewing a reflection of your inner world. Your mind is wrapped in, and protected by, your skull. Every physical human sense you hold can be activated by the organs that are also housed within the boundaries of it — your tongue, ears, eyes and nose. Your skin, which is responsive to touch, wraps around and protects it. Due to this correlation, skull carvings have the potential to assist you with self-reflection, personal discovery and transformation during your rituals and meditations. When you begin, choose one that is metaphysically representative of your current mental, emotional, spiritual and physical goals. For example, if you seek to become

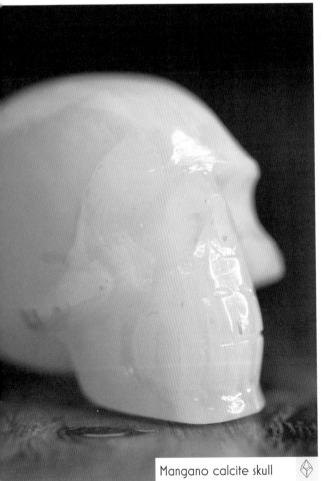

Mangano calcite skull

your most confident self and attract a continuous flow of success and abundance into your life, you may wish to use a skull carving in a solar plexus chakra crystal, such as Golden Healer quartz, for your ritual. Hold a vision of yourself within the skull form and picture your physical being absorbing the energy imprint that the crystal carries (this is a process that I call "energy fusion"). The purpose of this practice is to express the distinctive qualities the skull reflects back into you, thereby shifting your identity, perspective and behaviors to work in favor of your goals.

INTENTION

Preceding your work with crystal skulls, set your intention for the full embodiment of the essence or purpose that makes you whole and alive. Prepare to welcome change into all areas of your life — for the fragmentation and crumbling of old patterns and beliefs are crucial to the beginning stages of transformation. Releasing and rebuilding will be an ongoing theme in your energy fusion work. Trust the process and surrender attachments to old identities, especially in those you cling to in moments of raw vulnerability. This is when the light enters you and guides the way to self-actualization.

CONTACT THERAPY

Tracing over this shape with your fingers — over the exact areas where your sensory organs exist within your own skull — will activate your mirror neurons. Mirror neurons respond to actions and situations as if we were experiencing these ourselves. For example, these neurons will fire in your brain when you smell a fragrant flower and when you witness someone else smell the same flower. They are the source of your empathetic intelligence. In contact therapy, this tracing exercise lights up and rebuilds neural pathways that are beneficial to your growth, by captivating each of your physical senses. Start by gazing at the crystal skull and place your fingers on the top of it. As you perceive the shape beneath your fingertips, tune in to the tingling sensation that may begin to fizz over the top of your own head. If you don't feel this immediately, maintain your focus and give your brain a moment to make the connection. Follow your fingers down to trace the temple; then, over the location of the ears, eyes, nose and mouth. The tingling feeling you experienced at the top of your head may travel down to each respective zone on your face; music may play in your mind, and you may visualize colors, smell scents and even taste flavors — let it all rise. As you do this, pay attention to any messages you receive and the emotions you feel — honor the exercise as a special opportunity for self-discovery and take notes based on what you find. In this place of consciousness lies the golden information that will crack you open to shedding what does not serve, and owning your becoming.

ENVIRONMENT

Placing skull forms in your environment should be done intentionally, with a pointed focus on your desired healing outcome. Do you aspire to manifest a beneficial promotion in your career? Put a pyrite skull in your office. Are you inviting love and intimacy into your life? Set not one, but two rose quartz skulls in your bedroom. If you want to pursue amplification of every healing energy in your crystal collection, position a quartz crystal skull at the center of your crystal display. These are some simple examples of how to design your spaces with specific purposes in mind; however, there are an abundance of intentions you can address using different minerals, and even deliberate combinations of minerals. Align the crystal skull type(s), metaphysical properties and colors with the fulfillment of your most coveted intention; this considered approach will elevate the frequency of your space to one that attracts and amplifies the fusion of that intention with your personal energy. More importantly, align the crystal skull type, your intention and the function of the space you place the shape in, to create the perfect synergy for your efforts and manifestations. If your vision includes more than just yourself, match the number of skulls with the number of individuals involved. Every detail matters when working with crystal skulls for complete and total transformation.

DOUBLE-TERMINATED

Both naturally discovered and polished by hand, double-terminated crystals are the only shape on this list that are created by both the earth and human hands. Even more unique to this crystal form is the fact that naturally double-terminated crystals are sometimes polished to perfect them and repair any damage, establishing a collaboration between humans and nature. A doubly terminated crystal has two terminations or points: one on the top of the shaft and one on the bottom. Polished double-terminated shapes are always smooth in texture, while Mother Nature's double-terminated crystals can be both smooth and rough, depending on the mineral. Even the smoothest double-terminated crystals found naturally usually have rough spots and elevated lines that give them expressive character, and represent hundreds of millions of years of natural growth processes. This crystal shape is available in a vast selection of sizes, from pocket pieces to bold, colossal pieces that require a stand to display them — just take your pick based on your preferences! When you consider the magical qualities and metaphysical properties of double-

Double-terminated black chlorite
included phantom quartz

terminated crystals, and their ability to both direct and receive energy, there's a good chance you will want many in your collection – in a plethora of sizes and minerals.

Choosing to work with one, or multiple, double-terminated crystals in your rituals and meditations will prompt a noticeable shift within your internal and external worlds. As a bridge for both the transmission and receipt of energy, this shape is one of a kind in the manner it integrates the spiritual and the physical existences of your being. It is a symbol of interconnectedness, which activates remembrance that all aspects of self already exist as one, because they cannot exist without each other – everything you need is already within you and alignment with this fact is your natural right.

Utilizing this knowledge, consciously create gateways during your meditations between yourself and that which you are intent on manifesting. Mentally illustrate a golden light wave filling the gateway, and wrapping you and the subject of your vision in a loving cocoon. In this raised frequency and level of awareness are where inner peace, personal power and miracles are born. Adding to its allure, double-terminated crystal magic can unify anything, or anyone, in a spirited bond, creating opportunities for you to build fulfilling relationships, better communication, more wealth and abundance, oneness with your Higher Self and so much more. The choice is yours!

INTENTION

When working with double-terminated crystals, set your intention on sharpening your clarity of awareness surrounding the natural way energy flows into and through you. Acknowledge that this energy process is continual, and when used mindfully, with purpose, is a powerful doorway to receiving everything you dream. Remember to prioritize the energy exchange and embrace the notion that giving places you in a position to receive. By metamorphosing into a conscious conduit of the energy circulating within and all around you, you become the true master of your reality.

CONTACT THERAPY

Place double-terminated crystals on your body to create energy flow between your chakras. They are also empowering when simply held in the palm of your hand. By perceiving this shape as a wand, with electrical qualities and mystical capabilities, you can create a sense of playfulness, as well as worthiness and value within your self-perception. With the power of a "magic wand" in your hands, your mind may surge with dopamine as your imagination takes you back to your childhood – a time when you shamelessly believed anything and everything was possible, and you could envision anything into existence (especially by pointing your wand at it). While achieving dreams and goals is more complex than simply willing them into existence, that childhood version of yourself was on to something noteworthy about the process of manifestation: we achieve when we believe! Belief both opens the gateway and forms a bridge between you and the fulfillment of your aspirations. Therefore, the moment a double-terminated crystal is in your grip, activate this magic wand by rubbing it with your thumb, point it in the direction of your intention and in this childlike spirit begin calling in the golden light wave of your aspirations.

ENVIRONMENT

In their role as great connectors, double-terminated crystals can and should be placed anywhere in your environment in which you desire energy to flow more purposely. For example, homes with closed floor plans that prevent energy circulating from room to room, causing it to stagnate, can often become messy, stuffy and draining – which makes them the perfect candidates for energy reconfiguration using double-terminated crystal power. Place these crystals in spots where clutter tends to build, to immediately cut through stale energy and direct the mess into organized, dedicated locations. Anywhere that feels particularly disconnected from the rest of the home should have a double-terminated crystal intentionally placed to give and receive energy, to and from, the rest of the space. Remember, the orientation of the crystal matters: the terminations should point in the direction where you wish momentum to develop. You can even grid your entire home by placing a double-terminated crystal in each room, with all terminations pointing toward each other, thereby establishing a closed circuit of energy and communication. Couples may find it particularly beneficial to place a double-terminated wand between them when connecting, or having important heart-to-heart conversations. If there are specific places in which you connect with your significant other, plan to give those spaces the special double-terminated wand energy treatment to help heighten your bond.

CLEARING AND CHARGING CRYSTALS

Now that you know everything in the Universe vibrates with energy, including crystals, you are probably wondering how crystals can sustain their positive charge, given that we expose them to our own vibrational frequencies during our healing practices — and all things are affected by the frequencies of their environments. The fact is, just as it is essential to rebalance your personal energy to keep it at an optimal vibration, your crystals should be restored to their finest frequencies, too. There are a variety of methods to achieve this that involve either clearing or charging your crystals. However, before discussing my favorite methods for both, let's talk about the differences between clearing and charging, as they fulfill two very distinct needs. As this discussion progresses, you may well notice the peculiar parallels between clearing and charging your crystals, and clearing and charging your personal reality. They are, indeed, one and the same.

Clearing crystals is the act of removing any stored energetic impurities following their use in crystal healing practices, and after being handled by lots of people. This is therefore a good first step to take any time you add new specimens to your collection. From the mine where they were sourced to your living room display case, crystals come into contact with many different personalities, vibrations and possibly even intentions before making it safely to you.

Consider, also, what you are using your crystals for — are they serving you as a protective shield from unkind or draining people? Do you have them situated in a space with heavy WiFi to mitigate exposure to EMF? In circumstances like these, your crystals are absorbing energies that you are choosing to ward off for good reason. Eventually, they require a well-deserved break from their jobs, to ensure their continued maximum effectiveness and avoid the crystal equivalent of "burnout." You likely know that burnout is a consequence of constant expenditure of energy (or absorption of others' energy) without the necessary time spent alone for reflection and the release of all the extra energy, or worries, you are carrying. You can equate clearing your crystals to clearing your schedule to give yourself time to breathe. Both are important, but do you do them? If your answer to this question is usually "no," be grateful that, soon, your answer will be a resounding "yes" after you incorporate the Gem Sorcery Method into your way of life!

Charging generally happens post-clearing, and is meant to amplify the best energies and characteristics of your crystals; however, if your crystals have already been cleared and programmed, and you do not feel they are encumbered by any heavy energies, you do *not* need to clear them before charging them again. In fact, you can charge your crystals as many times as you want, even after harnessing their vibrations for several meditations. Use your intuition to determine when your crystals need to be cleared – you will know it when you feel it. Once your crystals are cleared, they will be in a beautiful state, filled with their most pure, inherent vibrational frequencies. But what if you wanted to increase their magic tenfold and thoroughly amplify their healing energies? Then charging them is the best way to go.

To get a better idea of what charging really means in the world of crystals, imagine how much better you feel when supporting your body with high-quality foods, daily sunshine, exercise and movement, while surrounding yourself with people who make you feel amazing: you become a version of yourself who wakes up with passion for the day ahead, radiating with luminous light and spreading contagious happiness with everyone you meet! You are *charged* up! By taking care of your crystals in the same manner that you tend to your connection with your Higher Self, you augment their ability to hold space for your healing and reflect your purposeful intention back to you. The illuminations we program our crystals with at the start of each Gem Sorcery meditation are magnified by crystal charging, too! (See the chapter on illuminations, page 83, for more on this.)

Now that you are aware of the differences between clearing and charging, let's look at some methods for each.

CHARGING YOUR CRYSTALS

The energy that crystals carry can help us access higher levels of awareness, intuition and manifestation. By charging your crystals, you are effectively charging your own consciousness with higher frequencies, making it easier for you to access these elevated states of being.

◇ **Sound vibrations:** Sound vibrations are a magnificent way to charge crystals. You can use singing bowls, tuning forks or even your own voice to create vibrations that resonate with the energy of your crystals. Simply hold your crystals in your hands and create a sound that feels harmonious with their energy.

Charging a large quartz with a singing bowl

◇ **Sunlight or moonlight:** Placing your crystals in direct sunlight or moonlight is a powerful way to charge them. Sunlight is energizing and invigorating, while moonlight is calming and nurturing. However, some crystals, such as amethyst and rose quartz, can fade in sunlight, so it's best to charge these crystals in moonlight.

◇ **Other crystals:** Some crystals are known for their ability to charge other crystals. Clear quartz is one of the most aligned crystals for this purpose, as it has a high energy vibration that can amplify the energy of other crystals. The same is true for selenite. To use this method, place your crystals on top of a clear quartz cluster or point, or a selenite charging plate, for a few hours.

⬠ **Intention:** One of my favorite ways to charge your crystals is with your own intention. Think carefully about what you wish to accomplish. When you're clear about your intention and have selected a crystal with properties that align with it, you are ready to begin. Hold the crystal in your hands and focus on infusing it with the energy of your intention. Speak your intention with bold confidence 3–5 times, visualizing your words floating toward the crystal and lighting it up with a vibrant glow. The crystal will now match the vibrational frequency of your words and intentions.

CLEARING YOUR CRYSTALS

Clearing your crystals allows them to return to their natural state, unaffected by any energies that they have come into contact with. It also offers you an opportunity to restore your own equilibrium and reaffirm your intentions in working with them.

⬠ **Running water:** Hold your crystal under cool, running water for a few minutes, visualizing any negative or stagnant energy being washed away. You may also choose to bring your crystal out into nature to submerge it in the waters at the edge of the ocean, a river, a stream or a lake, taking care not to lose it.

⬠ **Salt:** Place your crystal in a bowl of sea salt for several hours or overnight. However, do not use this method with certain soft or fragile crystals, such as apophyllite, as the salt may damage them.

⬠ **Smoke:** Use cleansing herbs such as sage to clear your crystals. Light a herb bundle, blow out the flame and let the smoke surround the crystal, visualizing the smoke carrying away any negativity as it envelops it in its thick covering.

⬠ **Sound:** Use a singing bowl, bell or other instrument to create sound vibrations that will clear your crystal. Hold the crystal close to the instrument and allow the sound to wash over it.

⬠ **Earth:** Bury your crystal in the soil for several hours or overnight, allowing it to connect with the grounding energy of the earth.

Clearing crystals with smoke

It's important to keep in mind that not all crystals can be cleared using the same methods. Before using any of the mentioned methods, be sure to research whether or not they are safe for your specific crystal. As stated, some crystals are sensitive to water or salt and could be damaged if subjected to those elements. Also, when burying your crystals, be sure to mark the location to prevent losing them. It is relevant to note that there are a couple of methods that can be used on most types of crystals. These are sound and smoke. Using sound vibrations or smoke from cleansing herbs can effectively clear your crystals, no matter their specific properties.

Charging and clearing your crystals is an essential aspect of crystal care that can enhance their power and amplify the energy of your own consciousness. By taking care of them in the same way that you attend to your Higher Self, you can create a powerful synergy between you and your crystals. Try out different methods of charging and see which ones resonate with you and your crystals the most. With regular charging, you'll be able to unlock the full potential of your crystals and access higher states of consciousness, healing and manifestation.

THE ILLUMINATIONS

In the Gem Sorcery Method, you will discover that each chakra has a shadow statement and an illumination statement assigned to it in Part 3. Similar to an affirmation, the illumination serves as the transmutation of shadow into light. The shadow statement reflects the energy of the chakra at its lowest vibration, while the illumination exemplifies the energy center at its highest vibration. While the shadow statement is offered for informational purposes only, to show the kind of thinking that accompanies each chakra when it is imbalanced, I will be asking you to work proactively with the illumination statement to help you move from a shadow state to an illumination mindset. With practice, the illumination mindset will come as naturally to you as breathing, filling you with wellbeing.

The objective here is to reframe your language and mindset surrounding the emotions and experiences governed by the specific chakra, and to embody the illumination until it is your truth. Words cast powerful spells through their vibrational energies and it is crucial to change how you speak about yourself to experience lasting change. Through repetition of the illuminations, you will break the pattern of limiting beliefs and establish new neural connections by feeling empowered emotions and having thoughts aligned with these.

The beauty of the illumination statements is that you can bring them with you anywhere you go, and retrieve them when you need a mindset shift during low-frequency states. When you catch yourself running a subconscious program, either in thoughts or behavior, a shift in mindset is a necessary first step in the cultivation of conscious awareness. This awareness makes it possible to continue to choose to change your mind, until the mindset becomes a natural part of who you are — and when your mindset is healthy, it directly corrects the balance of your energy centers, which guides your physical body into homoeostasis.

WORKING WITH THE ILLUMINATIONS

In the Gem Sorcery meditations in Part 3, the words and intention you will be focusing on will be those of the designated illumination statement. There is one illumination assigned to each chakra, making seven illumination statements in total, in which the ultimate objective is to open up a pathway for the release of subconscious energy blockages held in your mindset, followed by the assimilation of healthier, higher vibrational frequencies throughout the entirety of your energy body.

The crystals that you choose to work with for each chakra will not only carry the vibrations of the illumination statements at the end of your meditation practice, but also assume the role of a mirror, reflecting them back to you even when you are no longer practicing the meditations. Set these newly programmed crystals in a distinct place in your home, where you can go to bask in the energetic reflection of the illuminations whenever you need a reminder.

We will also tie physical sensations to the mindset shifts of the illuminations, taking intention setting with your crystals to a level you will only find in the Gem Sorcery Method. I will encourage you to explore the emotions involved with embodying the energy of your enlightened consciousness. The purpose of this is to raise your bodily awareness of what it will feel like when you fully step out of the shadow and transmute it to light — as if it spontaneously occurred, in the here and now. By using your mind and consciousness in this manner, you stimulate your brain to respond by releasing neurotransmitters (such as dopamine), which communicate with your nervous system, as well as control emotions, hormonal changes and other vital bodily functions that determine your health and wellbeing.

Sending your body into this powerful, parasympathetic state, while also programming your crystals, establishes an automatic association between your crystals and these uplifting chemical processes, thereby turning them into triggers for your best, most wonderful emotions. As a result, the crystals become easily accessible, unique tools for turning off your sympathetic nervous system and raising your vibrational frequency in times of anxiety or stress. All you need to do is pick up your favorite programmed crystal and open yourself up to the potential for greatness by restoring the emotion associated with the illumination statement. In this way, your crystal healing practice has the potential to dramatically shift your mind, body and spirit into their clearest, most coherent level of collaboration and communication yet.

Elestial smokey quartz

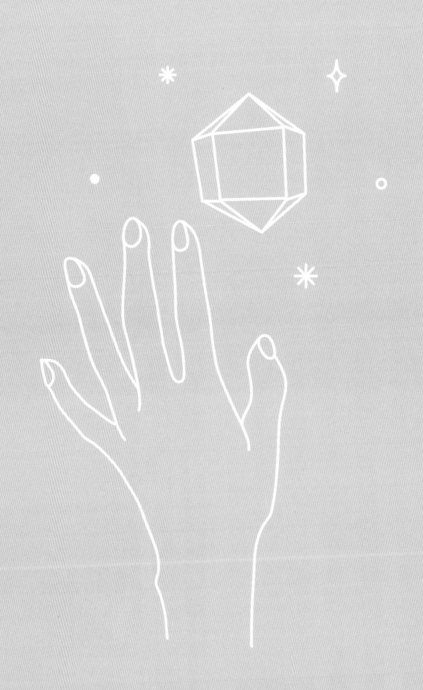

THE MEDITATIONS

Trust me when I say you will never experience any other guided meditations like the ones in Part 3 of this book. They are visceral, intense and mesmerizing, with the exceptional ability to transport you to alternate universes, while also developing a relationship of grounded self-awareness with your body. It sounds contradictory but is actually key to a successful sensory meditation to be out of your body, while also completely activated within it — spiritual travel and physical awareness, both accomplished at once.

These highly vivid guided meditations facilitate transformational travels through your chakras that establish a clear line of communication between your physical and subtle bodies. The meditations are specifically designed to make you fully present in your body as your sensory receptors, nervous systems, brain and endocrine system receive and transmit information, as well as aware of the effect these communications are having on your overall wellbeing (hint: the effect is positive). The purpose of these visualizations is not only to create a deep understanding of the vital, interconnectedness of the mechanisms of your body, but also to fortify the flow of communication, through mental suggestion and imagery. In collaboration with chakra-specific language, color psychology, relevant emotions and environments, the guided meditations move — as well as balance — your energy for peak vitality.

THE MEDITATIONS AND THE SENSES

Dendritic Golden Healer quartz flame

In the root to throat chakra meditations, one of the five senses will be activated to create complete presence in the body, grounding chaotic thoughts and helping you to develop sensory associations with higher frequency mindsets.

During the sixth meditation, on pages 214–15, you will have the opportunity to uplevel the karmic DNA passed on through your lineage and release patterns that do not serve your highest manifestation of self.

The seventh meditation, on pages 234–5, guides you to a state of unity consciousness, where all things are one, and no thing exists. In this space, there are no fears, worries or doubts – no past or future – because you *are* the eternal present.

After completing all seven Gem Sorcery guided meditations, mind, body and spirit attain coherence. You and your energy are liberated in space–time.

IMAGERY AND SOUNDS

The meditations will invite you to visualize particular scenarios and engage your imagination and your senses in them. In addition, vibrant, intentional crystal photography accompanies each individual chakra described in Part 3, and formulates a visual experience meant to stimulate your imagination and provide brilliant subjects for you to explore if you wish, while engaging in the meditations and beyond.

Bring your focus to the photos and adventure through their colors and details. They may seem to come alive as you delve into their naturally psychedelic features. Magnify the effect by tracing your finger over the edges of each crystal featured in the images. Not only will this activate your sense of touch, it will bring you into a more hypnotic state where your mind frees itself from ruminating thoughts.

The guided meditations have been set to original crystal singing bowl music, individually recorded for each of the energy centers and their unique vibrations (see Resources, page 248). The main mission of the sound healing tracks is to deliver high frequency tones for your physical body to match through the process of entrainment – the natural synchronization and alignment of your body with these rhythms. Your body is in a constant state of vibration and has the capacity to completely switch its oscillations in response to an outside pulse. Doesn't this fact instantly inspire you to get serious about the "vibes" you accept into your life? It sure does bring new meaning to the phrase, "good vibes only"!

RELEASE

When you work through the energy blockages in your chakra centers via the meditations, repressed memories and emotions are likely to bubble up to the surface. Don't be alarmed by what you discover, as the only way out is through. What I mean by this is, having conscious awareness of the experiences you persistently hide in the depths of your subconscious mind, is the only way to dismantle them from having any further negative impact on your wellbeing.

It may feel uncomfortable and your brain might start sending signals to shut down the sensations by restoring them back to your subconscious. If, or when, this occurs, create a dialogue with the painful memories or voices that arise. Ask them questions and do your best to understand their source, as well as their purpose. You can ask questions like, "What is the purpose of keeping you around? What will my life look and feel like once I forgive you? What do I need to do to honor you, then say goodbye?"

Be gentle on yourself and take a break from the work if you need to. Breathe deeply, and reassure your body and mind that you are not re-experiencing the painful memory — you simply want to understand it to heal it. The most important thing you can do in these moments is take small steps forward and move away from states of disempowerment. Do not linger in cyclical, negative thoughts and do not continue to repress your memories and/or emotions. Use a positive trigger such as a crystal or essential oil blend to reposition your mind toward progressive breakthrough. If you need professional help to tackle what surfaces, please seek this.

PREPARING TO MEDITATE

Please ensure that you do the meditations in the order they are presented — beginning at the root chakra and ending at the crown chakra. It is helpful to do each meditation several times before graduating to the next because, essentially, you are building the groundwork for total energy alignment from bottom to top. To augment your meditation experience, download the guided meditation and sound healing album offered with your purchase of the book (see Resources, page 248). Allow my voice to carry you through the process with your eyes closed and your heart open.

Before you begin meditating, turn off any devices (other than the accompanying audio, if using) and make yourself comfortable in a place where you will not be disturbed. Take a moment or two to settle yourself. If you have one or more of the crystals featured in the chakra meditation, hold them in your hands. You are not required to have any of the tools featured in the book to participate in the meditations, as they are intended to activate your senses using the boundless nature of your mind and imagination; however, the tools heighten the physical experience and bring you to the next level of your healing journey. Close your eyes if you wish, or soften your gaze if you are gazing at the crystal imagery that accompanies the chakra.

At the end of the meditation, take your time to reflect and record your findings in your Gem Sorcery journal before you go about your daily life.

Celestite

PREPARE
TO BEGIN

Wellness is a lifelong commitment. The practice of Gem Sorcery is a ritual for building new habits that will genuinely change your life. In order to have this powerful effect, rituals are best repeated and integrated into a routine that supports your evolution. Gem Sorcery is no exception. This ritual should continue to transform with you, as you peel back the many fine layers of your subconscious mind, and reveal the aspects of your story that continue to shape who you are today, whether for better or for worse. The deeper you are willing to go, the closer you will arrive at the incarnation of your true nature, your Higher Self.

There may be moments of discomfort, which tempt you to return to the safety of your comfort zone — where doubt, old patterns and behaviors, guilt, blame and other familiar emotions reside. When you live in these states for a long time, you can become chemically, mentally and emotionally dependent on them, and it may be challenging to leave them behind. They once protected and defined you; however, much like an old friend that you've grown apart from — it is okay to say goodbye. Setting this boundary is an investment in your future.

Although it may hurt at times, you will look back on how far you came and realize exactly why you chose yourself and your Inner Child so many times. So, when the discomfort of the unknown arises, recognize the emotion, thank it for its perspective, trust that where you are going is home — and take a single step forward. That one step is called discipline, and it is all you need to keep progressing when motivation is fleeting.

Last but not least, when actively participating in Gem Sorcery, always come back to the purpose and goal: the integration of your mind, body and spirit. Keep all three aspects of yourself at the forefront of your awareness, so each receives the necessary intention, and attention, throughout the process.

Correlate every exercise with its respective piece of the puzzle. For example, when you feel a crystal against your skin, acknowledge that your physical body is receiving activation, and when your mindset is directed toward an empowering thought, appreciate that your brain is making new neural connections.

The relationship every action has with your overall interconnected being will begin to make perfect sense to you, and you will be in constant flowing communication with all aspects of self. If it takes more time and practice for you to get there, that is okay!

Keep going and continue learning. Then, keep going some more. Again, this book is not meant to provide you with an overnight transformation. It is intended to be your guide through the work you do. The Gem Sorcery Method is continuous and ever-evolving – your transformation and healing are, too.

Phantom quartz crystals

PAUSE AND BREATHE

Before jumping into the next part of the book, take a moment to check in with yourself. Beginning the Gem Sorcery journey is an agreement – one you make with yourself – to accept the responsibility of being the natural leader and creator of your reality. With each meditation and sensory experience, you are choosing to release the programming of your past and create space for an entirely new definition of what it means to be you. You may have heard the saying that "freedom isn't free" and, to an extent, this is true. Your liberation into the natural, highest version of self requires commitment to your remembering. It compels you to trust.

Whether it feels like a good time to start, or not, the now moment is the only moment. One decision that you are ready, is the only thing you need to make a change. Your hands hold this book between them, because your spirit led the way.

1. Confirm with your mind – your consciousness – that you are ready.

2. Feel the knowing in your body.

3. Take one long, deep breath. This is your first exercise in alignment of mind, body and spirit.

4. Now that you are here, you are ready.

PART 3

BALANCING THE CHAKRAS WITH GEM SORCERY

SHADOW

"Scarcity and lack dominate my perception of life, leading me to believe I am neither enough, nor will I ever have the stability to create the life I want — love and success will forever remain a dream, and only a dream."

ILLUMINATION

"As the creator of my reality, I live in my strength and consistently take action to embody my best self. I am deserving of a beautiful, happy, safe and secure life — my personal power is more than enough to generate and magnetize this truth."

ROOT CHAKRA

Key Themes:
Grounding and foundations

Element:
Earth

Color:
Red

Color Psychology:
Motivation, willpower, strength, leadership, confidence, passion, survival and physical vitality

Sense: Smell

Utilize your sense of smell to indulge in the fragrances of the sensory tools described in this section, which are linked to the energies of the root chakra and the earth element. Inhale the fragrance of the listed flowers, create potpourri with the herbs and diffuse the essential oils.

Herbs:
Ashwagandha, licorice root, dandelion root, ginger root, purple coneflower

Flowers:
Poppy, cactus, borage, hibiscus, peony

Essential Oils:
Vetiver, myrrh, frankincense, sandalwood, patchouli

Environment:
Dense wet forest after rainfall, where the musky scent of freshly sprouted mushrooms wafts through the air.

Body Awareness:
Legs, feet, knees, base of spine, testes, immune system, skeletal and muscular systems

Subtle Body Auric Layer:
Etheric body

SEVEN ROOT CHAKRA CRYSTALS

The following crystals all support the illumination of the root chakra, in a manner that applies to each of the subsequent energy centers, too. Think of these crystals as reminders of the person you strive to be and the dedication required for transforming aspects of your identity that are no longer in alignment with the best version of yourself. Calling in these seven characteristics begins with your commitment: the crystals will work with, and for, you as you set your intentions on balancing this chakra.

1. Stibnite
2. Smokey quartz
3. Black tourmaline
4. Red limonite quartz
5. Spessartine garnet
6. Hematite quartz
7. Vanadinite

BLACK TOURMALINE
Protection

Black tourmaline creates a line of defense from negativity, energy zaps, naysayers and mal-intent. When shedding people, places, ideas or things that do not contribute to our growth, resistance may appear; with the protective energy of black tourmaline, trust that this is simply a small challenge to overcome.

HEMATITE QUARTZ
Grounding

Hematite clears the way to return peacefully to the body whenever overwhelm takes over. Regaining spiritual, mental and physical homoeostasis is requisite to successfully crafting the path of our purpose in this lifetime. When our mind mirrors the grounded, beautiful and magical life we want to live, our reality reflects our vision.

RED LIMONITE QUARTZ
Stability

Red limonite quartz facilitates a stable environment in which it is possible to continuously improve and grow. With this foundational energy, we act from a place of empowerment, rather than doubt and fear. Chaos and confusion are things of the past as we establish the pillars of our success.

SMOKEY QUARTZ
Support

Smokey quartz reminds us of the many ways we are supported in life and in our endeavors. Upon making the decision to change, we signal to the Universe that we are ready to receive and be held through our transformation. The nurturing energy of smokey quartz encourages our Inner Child to trust the process of picking ourselves up and making progress after we stumble.

SPESSARTINE GARNET
Courage
Spessartine garnet seeks to usher in our bravest, boldest self when taking risks and jumping into the unknown. Courage takes us to greater heights, where fear is diminished by the healing power of finally releasing the old karmic energy that once held us back.

STIBNITE
Strength
Stibnite carries the energy of resilience, offering us the opportunity to stand strong in the face of adversity. Maintaining steadfast optimism when cynicism shows up along our journey will be the difference between giving up and proving to ourselves that we can achieve mastery of our life.

VANADINITE
Discipline
Vanadinite helps to amplify our willingness to wake up every day with passion and determination. Transforming into a stronger, more grounded and self-aware person requires faithfulness to the goal, every single day. The fire spirit of vanadinite helps stoke the flame of motivation deep within us.

ROOT CRYSTAL SUBSTITUTES
Black kyanite, black onyx, bloodstone, pyrite, red carnelian, red jasper, red tiger's eye

CREATING BALANCE

Once you've chosen your crystal and set your intentions for optimizing your root chakra, certain signs will show whether you have achieved balance in your first energy center, or whether it remains imbalanced.

MANIFESTATIONS OF BALANCE

Mental	Grounded	Open-mindedness	Confidence	Self-awareness	Assertiveness
Physical	Long, smooth muscles free from tension	Confident body language	Financial stability	Physical fitness and vitality	Strong immune system
Emotional	Safety	Security	Relaxation	Trust	Satisfaction
Spiritual	Grounded in physical reality	Sense of belonging

MANIFESTATIONS OF IMBALANCE

Mental	Rigidity	Offended	Pessimism	Greed	Impatience
Physical	Musculoskeletal pain	Poor posture	Lethargy or hyperactivity	Lack of abundance and stability	Frequent illness
Emotional	Fear	Aggression	Anxiety	Distrust	Lack of power
Spiritual	Head in the clouds	Inability to relate

THE ROOT CHAKRA IS THE FOUNDATION

The root chakra is the first energy center of the body. To gain a visual understanding of it, imagine the roots of a tree: the healthier the roots, the stronger the foundation for the rest of the tree to thrive. Without healthy roots, the tree may wither and topple, whereas a healthy root system allows the tree to absorb vital minerals and sufficient water. The result is a tall tree with plentiful leaves. This healthy, stable tree is magnetic — it coexists harmoniously with the surrounding natural environment, in reciprocity and connection. It produces cleaner air, reduces flooding impacts and creates healthier soil; essentially, healthy trees with healthy roots make the world a better, lovelier place for all beings. And the same is true for people with healthy, balanced root chakras: they are stronger, happier, more secure and create from a place of trust and abundance.

They have stable relationships and feel secure enough to give to others, while also maintaining healthy boundaries.

The root chakra truly is foundational, with a healthy first energy center expressing the strong and stable qualities of the Divine Masculine. As the name suggests, it is the *root* of your existence, governing the foundations of who you are, how you survive and your connection to the primal, physical aspects of self. This includes your capacity for connection, love for your body, your proficiency in creating (and maintaining) financial abundance, your energy levels, and your

Vanadinite

ability to remain grounded in all situations. In a testament to its vital nature, the first energy center influences and impacts every one that comes after it; if it is imbalanced, one is likely to encounter hyperactivity, or underactivity, in all seven chakras. Therefore, when doing full body energy work, beginning at the root is key for achieving optimal alignment.

Your legs, knees, ankles and feet and your entire musculoskeletal system form the groundwork for bodily movement and support, and are the body parts most closely associated with the functional quality of the first energy center. Also linked to this chakra are the testes of the male reproductive system, which produce testosterone — responsible for muscle and bone development, as well as fertility. Ailments and chronic pain within these areas of the body may be messengers of a misaligned root chakra, in need of energetic balancing. It is important to note that addressing the physical expression of pain via practices such as bodywork, stretching and acupuncture will likewise contribute to the proper functioning of the first energy center.

Smokey quartz

Being outside and at one with nature is a simple activity that also benefits these individuals in a way that feeds their spirits and makes them feel whole.

People with healthy root chakras are usually comfortable in their bodies, steadfast and confident. They often enjoy a stable income, or easily attract the kind of financial increases that afford them the freedoms of safety and creation — humans are more likely to reach their full potential if they are not struggling to get by and can seek out those activities that bring them joy and fulfillment, rather than only doing what they must to survive. (This links to the fact that the center for creativity — the sacral chakra — and then the center for confidence and potential — the solar plexus chakra — come right after the first energy center, respectively.) Individuals with a strong root chakra have a platform that enables them to trust, which eventually leads them to express, communicate and open up to the possibility for love and even spiritual expansion. After all, the physical body must be taken care of and the worldly existence tended to before we will have the bandwidth to reach true union with the Universal Consciousness.

People with strong and activated root chakras tend to gravitate toward stable careers, such as those of healthcare workers, doctors and nurses. Others who are deeply in tune with the earth may become stewards of the land in the form of farmers, conservationists, sustainable home builders and architects. Another route that these individuals may take is that of therapy; being a therapist allows someone with a healthy root chakra to create safety for others, thereby providing a sense of accomplishment and strength in themselves, because they understand the value of advocacy.

When considering the factors that influence the condition of the energy centers, and especially the first, it is critical to explore the most foundational years of your life — your childhood. Much of what you experience and learn at this time becomes embedded in the subconscious mind and continues to run as programs that influence who you are today. Your habits, behaviors, perspectives, thought processes and level of self-awareness are wired into you by environmental factors and exposures. Revisiting our tree root metaphor, imagine what might happen if a tree did not have the proper environment to grow in? Ultimately, our tree would not have the foundation to become the best tree it could be. Similarly, if neglect, lack of trust, fear and anger overwhelmed your childhood environment, due to negative interactions with family or overexposure to mainstream media, for example, those negative emotions may perpetuate themselves and seep into every aspect of your adult life — your external world might mirror your unaddressed, subconscious shadows. However, if it is balanced, safe and stable, then it is conducive to flourishing growth, grounded energy, safety and a regulated nervous system. In turn, your transition into adulthood is likely to be smoother, as a result of learning a healthy way of relating with the world.

The beautiful thing is that, despite the past, it is never too late to rewire your mind, body and spirit. You can choose a path of transformation through intentional effort and practice. Most importantly, by making the subconscious conscious, you bring the trapped energy of the body into a state of movement and flow, where it can then be fully discovered and understood. Consciousness is the bridge of communication between repressed or forgotten memories and the physical, mental, emotional or spiritual symptoms that occur as a result. The integration of consciousness with unconscious memories is vital for the root chakra, as it houses many of our core childhood memories. This is significant because, up until the age of three, the brain develops an excess of neural connections that are then pruned or strengthened, based on use and environmental input. This lays the groundwork for how our brain processes information throughout adulthood. As we lack conscious recollection of our experiences at this age, it is important to foster openness and communication in this energy center. As the foundational energy center and the source of your energetic life force, creating awareness and movement in the root chakra initiates the opening of the portal to alignment. When this layer of your aura becomes more whole through the retrieval of soul pieces that were lost or broken after traumatic childhood experiences, the subsequent layers of the subtle body are primed for their evolution. We therefore begin at the root chakra, triggering the sense of smell and thereby generating new associations, and neural connections, that align with the illumination of this chakra.

Stibnite

REWRITING YOUR STORY

After bringing subconscious patterns into the light of consciousness, the next step is to take action that stops these in their tracks and establishes a new path to walk toward the reality you do want — despite what anyone else has to say about it. One of the greatest lessons I learned on my journey through healing chronic illness, is that people will always speak their perspectives and opinions into your life. If their influence is negative and you do not filter out their energy before it settles in your subconscious, you may believe you are powerless to make positive change. Children are impressionable, with sponge-like brains. What minerals and nutrients are to a tree, words and ideas are to a child's consciousness.

Hematite quartz

When I was a child, I became sick frequently. The story told for me was that I had "a terrible immune system." I heard this statement so often that I believed my body did not function properly and that my immune system worked against me. Having a "bad" immune system became a defining characteristic for me and my "normal." My lifestyle, environment and food choices were never analyzed as a potential source of my frequent bouts of illness, despite the fact that these habits are learned in childhood and oftentimes stay with us into adulthood. Over and over again, I heard the same old tale — that I would forever be ill and had to learn to live with it. Hearing that I would never be safe in my first home, my body, was scary and depressing. My root chakra became blocked as I lost hope in, and connectedness with, my body. Thankfully, when older, I found myself questioning the validity of that curse. By that point, I understood that everything is energy and all encounters involve an exchange. Continuing to do everything the way I always did would beget the same results, while making new, different decisions would change the cycle and create new outcomes. So, I ditched the story, changed my habits and my mindset, and invested in my body's ability to heal. It was the best, most transformative step I took in my entire life up until then.

Other traumas and experiences can also have a negative impact on the wellbeing of your first energy center. These experiences include, but are not limited

Red limonite quartz

to, being a child of divorce, natural disasters, growing up in extreme poverty, witnessing violence between family members, being a victim of violence and childhood neglect by parents and/or caretakers. Each of these scenarios is unique and the healing process is highly individualized, but one thing is constant: the importance of having a safe place, person, group of people or tool to receive you, as you learn to come face to face with, and forgive, the realities of your upbringing. It is also vital to hold an image of yourself in a state of integration and understanding, embodying the illumination of your darkness, to which end there is an exercise on page 115.

Smell is also linked to the grounding nature of the first energy center. By activating the sense of smell, we trigger a primal source of memory and human connection. Smell is tied to the survival of the human species, allowing us to select partners and determine whether food is safe to consume. It is also one of the first senses to develop after conception (after touch and at around the same time as taste), and remains one of the strongest senses throughout our most formative years. Mother and baby are deeply connected via smell – a baby can sniff out its mother's breastmilk. Therefore, it is logical to associate the energy center in charge of security and survival with the human sense responsible for establishing these connections. Unlike any other sense, smell information is sent directly through the olfactory system to limbic system brain structures such as the hypothalamus, amygdala and hippocampus. Each of these is directly correlated to memories and emotional responses. Consequently, smells activate memories. The tools in this chapter give you the means for making *intentional*, high frequency, emotional connections with the smell sense activators, to effortlessly recall the energy of the root chakra illumination in your daily life.

Marrying the invigorating activation of the smell sense with the root chakra illumination is the amplifying energy of the seven root chakra crystals listed earlier.

HEALING POWERS

Each of the seven root chakra crystals represents a fundamental characteristic that upholds the overall illumination mindset. These crystals will not only serve as catalysts for raising your frequency in moments where you find yourself entertaining the shadow mindset for too long, but will physically raise the vibration of your aura as it interacts with the crystals' own stable electromagnetic fields. Mind, body and spirit collaborate in a harmonious flow of energy, where each is energized and communicating at its highest level of efficacy and flow – because each is tended to with intention and love.

Crystals are most frequently associated with the root chakra when they are the color red, but as you can see in the imagery, it is not necessary for them to be red in order to balance the first energy center. When I left university because of my illness, I reunited with my childhood crystal collection and each crystal spoke to me in a way it never did before. I discovered that crystals related to the earth, and thus the root chakra, were often black and even very dense in weight. This made sense because heavier crystals are the representation of grounded energy, counterbalancing the esoteric nature of the upper chakras and the "head in the clouds" state of being that occurs when you are too heavily invested in those.

The root and the crown chakras may seem like polar opposites in energetic purpose, with their respective dark- and light-colored crystal associations – as if symbolizing the physical element of earth versus the formless Universal Consciousness, and their locations of bottom-most and top-most – yet they are equally important on the path to alignment. While root chakra crystals may appear to be opposites to those linked with the crown chakra, they perfectly complement them through magnetic polarity. Crystals of the root chakra can be dark, round in shape, raw in nature, dense and earthy, associated with masculine qualities such as drive, courage and strength, and with earthly, external pursuits such as monetary wealth; in contrast to the light, airy crystals of the higher chakras, which embody the energy of everything and nothing all at the same time.

Should you find yourself experiencing excessive fear, lacking trust in people and the world around you, or struggling to care about your purpose in this life, you are likely living in a state of energetic underactivity in the first energy center. Alternatively, you may find you are driven by greed, exist in the state of a "never enough" attitude, are hostile and aggressive, and hyperactive – the telltale signs of an overactive root chakra. It is important to find the balanced manifestation of this type of energy, which is the masculine in its most embodied and natural form. This looks like security, trust, self-awareness, confidence, drive and healthy assertiveness. The masculine and feminine energies reside in all people and require one another to thrive. Garnering sound masculine qualities in the root chakra is vital, whatever your gender. Because this energy center is so deeply impacted and developed by the childhood years, root chakra work is needed by almost everyone to find resolution to the long-held and often hidden blockages that may impact us today. By balancing this chakra, you take personal responsibility for lessening the load on future generations, while also bringing resolution to the little you that has been waiting for this healing moment all along.

When dealing with an overactive root chakra, color therapy can help bring more subtlety into your world. The color blue is the opposite of red, thereby making it beneficial to incorporate blue clothing, crystals and environments into your routine. Rather than removing red entirely, combine blue *with* red to ease any physical, mental, emotional or spiritual repercussions of this imbalance. Blue reminds us to make slow, intentional moves and think before taking action if we tend to make decisions in haste out of strong and/or angering triggers, for example.

Black tourmaline

Of course, if you need more root chakra activation because yours is sluggish, then the more red in your environment the better. Sprinkle red around you everywhere you go and feel the heat of passion that you need!

Root chakra balancing is deep, committed and sacred work. When clearing and rewiring years upon years of obstructive neurological connections, habitual thoughts and painful memories, there is no express train to take you from point A to point B. In other words, you must make the choice to face your past, fully rewrite your narrative, and take control of the direction of your life. It will be ugly and painful, yet euphoric and empowering at the same time. You will see yourself for who you truly are, as you shed ideas and thoughts given to you by others. You will recall traumas that subconsciously shaped your life, giving you the opportunity to deconstruct their power and consciously redefine your truth.

By balancing your root chakra, you become the ultimate creator of your internal and external world, weaving empowered existence through everything, and everyone, you encounter. Given the proper tools, authentically embodying the root chakra mindset will become second nature for you.

Spessartine garnet

INHALE AND GROW

This exercise flips the narrative from "product of my circumstances" to "evolving through my experiences." It also activates the root chakra's grounding sense of smell.

1. First, ground yourself mentally and physically. If you wish, make yourself a soothing cup of licorice and dandelion root tea by steeping 1 tbsp of licorice root and 1 tbsp of dandelion root in hot water for 10 minutes, to sip while you reflect.

2. Referring to the list of herbs and essential oils on page 99, prepare your space with a suitable fragrance. You could scatter the petals of peonies around you, place drops of sandalwood or vetiver in a diffuser, or burn frankincense or myrrh resin in an incense burner. (Do not make physical contact with the flame, hot bowl, or burning charcoal and resin. Please practice fire safety and do not leave hot items unattended.)

3. Intuitively select one of the crystals. Hold this or gaze at it.

4. Now ask yourself, "Who would I be if I was always supported, loved and safe? Who would I be if I was living in my highest purpose? What impact would I have on the world if I transmuted my pain into the equivalent amount of light and magic?"

5. Write down your answers to these questions in your Gem Sorcery journal and choose, in each moment, to act from the embodiment of *that* person — and send love to the child inside who feels unsafe or unloved.

ROOT CHAKRA MEDITATION

Create a soothing cup of herbal tea using root chakra herbs or diffuse essential oils for a calming atmosphere. Decorate with recommended flowers to amplify the fragrances swirling around you. Expect to hold grounding root chakra crystals in your palms for Earth connection. Prepare to begin.

Welcome to your root chakra meditation. Take a seat. Find yourself in a cross-legged position, or lie flat on your back with your knees bent, the bare soles of your feet making direct contact with the ground beneath you. Wrap yourself in your blanket and reach into the space of your being that feels deeply and unconditionally safe and held. Ensure that you are comfortable, as comfortable as you should feel when held tightly and warmly in your mother's womb. Warm, nurtured, surrounded by the distant voices of loved ones.

Now, bring your awareness to the heaviness of your lower body – your feet touching the ground, the pressure of your thighs counteracted by the support of your knees and ankles, all the way up to your perineum, where the glowing red energy of the root chakra resides.

Reach for your root chakra crystal and analyze how it feels in your hand, while still maintaining awareness of your first energy center. The weight of it is noticeable in contrast to the lightness of your fingers, and the palm of your hand. Transfer this heaviness into your perineum and allow it to sink you deeper and deeper into union with the earth below you.

Now, you are connected. Mother Earth supports you with all of her love.

Imagine roots beginning to form at the base of your spine, down through your perineum, sinking into the earth. These roots are your umbilical cord, attached to the placenta, where you retrieve all of your vital minerals and nutrition while in the womb of the greatest mother. Without expectation, she provides. Giving and giving, as the miracle of life continues to develop within your body, your home.

One day, while still a tiny sapling with developing roots, you experience your first sense of smell, giving you the unique opportunity to connect with, and understand, the world around you. Surrounded by a field full of flowering herbs, you inhale the scent of the budding flowers of hibiscus and peonies – subtle yet overpowering all the same.

The colors are so vibrant, mostly warm and red. You melt even deeper into the earth, in a state of pure reverence.

You are a brand new tree, forming in the most well-kept, well-loved garden, receiving all of the intentional effort of a wonderful nurturing woman. You recognize her by the smell of patchouli, vetiver and sandalwood essential oils. As she waters your soil and adores your leaves, she repeats this affirmation:

"As the creator of my reality, I live in my strength and consistently take action to embody my best self. I am deserving of a beautiful, happy, safe and secure life – my personal power is more than enough to generate and magnetize this truth."

She repeats it so often, you begin to repeat it, too. Clutching your crystal tighter, close your eyes and repeat: "As the creator of my reality, I live in my strength and consistently take action to embody my best self. I am deserving of a beautiful, happy, safe and secure life – my personal power is more than enough to generate and magnetize this truth."

You open your eyes to realize you are a taller, mature tree looking out upon this inspiring garden, where the scent of flowers fills your consciousness. You feel the warm sensation of a body press against you and arms wrap around you. It's her. Giving thanks to you for your contribution to her life and her garden. She is significantly older now, yet as vibrant and loving as ever, still leaving a trail of patchouli and sandalwood fragrance in her wake.

As she unwraps her arms from around you, she places a crystal upon your roots. It is the same crystal you are holding in your hand.

She repeats: "As the creator of my reality, I live in my strength and consistently take action to embody my best self. I am deserving of a beautiful, happy, safe, and secure life – my personal power is more than enough to generate and magnetize this truth."

Her words stay with you as she slowly walks away. For the rest of your life, you will hear these words and repeat them, continuing to strengthen your conviction in them every day. As you gently emerge from this meditation, your crystal reminds you of this powerful truth, every time you see it, reach for it and hold it.

SACRAL CHAKRA

Key Themes:
Pleasure, creativity
and nourishment

Element:
Water

Color:
Orange

Color Psychology:
Creativity, adventure,
freedom, optimism,
motivation, fun, strength

Sense: Taste

Make time in your day to savor
your food. When the body is
nourished, the mind is enriched
and the spirit invigorated.
Examine the parallels between
the food that nourishes you and
the aspects of your life that do,
or do not, nourish you. Are you
strengthened and energized
by what you consume? Does it
truly nourish and fulfill you?

Herbs:
Rosemary, pepper, damiana

Flowers:
Red roses, orange tulips

Foods:
Oranges, carrots, sweet potatoes

Environment:
Surrounded by the womb-like
energy and shapes of orange
flowers, opening and closing in
a process of seasonal birth and
death. A small stream trickles —
although gentle now, heavy rains
sometimes transform it into a
creek. You imagine the sounds of
the rushing water in contrast to
the gentle bubbling of the stream.

Body Awareness:
Reproductive organs (e.g.
womb and ovaries), lymphatic
system, kidneys, bladder, bowels,
lower back, pelvis, hips

Subtle Body Auric Layer:
Emotional body

SEVEN SACRAL CHAKRA CRYSTALS

These warming crystals are wonderful for nourishing the illumination of the sacral chakra.

1. Peach moonstone
2. Copper
3. Orange calcite
4. Sardonyx
5. Honey calcite
6. Golden topaz
7. Amber

AMBER

Expression

Amber provides the energy of acceptance and non-judgment when we begin to walk the path of creation. Amber's warm spirit and comforting, golden orange color is the equivalent of a big hug from someone we love, while they encourage us to "go get 'em, tiger." That kind of support is irreplaceable when committing to absolute self-expression.

COPPER

Passion and creativity

Copper activates the point where the subconscious meets the conscious mind with energy and passion. Copper encourages us to express ourselves creatively, supporting our conscious transformation and sending waves of positivity out into the world around us.

GOLDEN TOPAZ

Self-confidence

Golden topaz ignites the self-belief required to support our transformation. We are worthy of the great things that arise when we fully embody the energy of our truth, when we love ourselves unconditionally. With its orange hued and bright, reflective qualities, golden topaz is equal to the epic light we give out to the world when we trust we are exactly who, and where, we want to be.

HONEY CALCITE

Childlike wonder

Honey calcite is a bright reminder of the magic available in each moment, if we are willing to acknowledge it. If seen with the eyes of a child, there is abundant possibility and joy in everything we touch, see and do. When in a state of admiration and gratitude, our vibration begins to attract the visions we hold for our most vibrant existence. In this way, honey calcite assists us in manifesting our reality with childlike wonder.

ORANGE CALCITE

Motivation

Orange calcite builds upon the foundation of vitality with the energy of amplification and action. Motivation is the movement that keeps us going when challenges arise and in moments when we may feel like giving up on our path to progression. With its stunning bright hues, orange calcite incites the spirit to spring into action and dance magically through the waves of life.

PEACH MOONSTONE

Fertility and sexuality

Peach moonstone is a gentle yet effective activator of the Divine Feminine energy of creation. Birth, death and rebirth are inherent cycles through which we evolve into our unique self. Whether this is through the evolution of birthing a new human into the world or a form of self-expression, it is the bringing about of something that once did not exist. Creation is the driving force of the Universe. Tap into its fertile soil with the energy of peach moonstone.

SARDONYX

Vitality

The fiery red and orange aesthetic of sardonyx represents the potent internal energy it births within those who utilize it in their healing practices. Sardonyx fans the flame of life force energy that serves as the catalyst for strength and action. Sufficient vitality is the key to positive growth and change, and sardonyx is a tremendous inspiration.

SACRAL CRYSTAL SUBSTITUTES

Carnelian, fire opal, orange kyanite, orange selenite, peach stilbite, tangerine quartz, vanadinite

CREATING BALANCE

Once you've chosen your crystals and set your intentions for balancing your sacral chakra, take note of the signs that show whether you have achieved balance in your second energy center, or whether it remains imbalanced.

MANIFESTATIONS OF BALANCE

Mental	Open-mindedness	Inspiration	Creativity	Positivity	Abundance
Physical	Fertility	Limber	Regular bowel movements	Efficient detox pathways	Healthy libido
Emotional	Sensuality	Comfort	Optimism	Empathy	Desire
Spiritual	Tuned in to the Universal Flow	Trust in the process

MANIFESTATIONS OF IMBALANCE

Mental	Judgment	Lack of inspiration	Rigidity	Disconnect	Suppressed
Physical	Lower back pain	Urinary tract infection	Menstrual pain	Low or excessive libido	Reproductive organ ailments
Emotional	Lack of hope	Lust	Withdrawal	Shame	Bitterness
Spiritual	Fear of change	Disconnect from Inner Child

THE SACRAL CHAKRA CRADLES CREATION

The sacral chakra is our seat of pleasure, creativity, emotion and intimacy. It occupies a formidable yet vulnerable space just below the naval and is represented by the color orange. This second energy center governs the womb and sexual organs and surrounding areas such as the kidneys, bladder, bowels, hips and pelvis — all areas of the body that tend to carry pent-up emotions. It is the source of energetic flow, where embers of vitality swirl about and ignite flames of passion and manifestation.

The second energy center deals with all things birth and rebirth, as well as the acceptance of, and respect for, death as a natural part of the life cycle. When balanced and fully open, the sacral chakra generates joy for life, impactful creativity, clear self-expression, emotional balance and a healthy drive for sexual contact. There is no judgment of self and the human existence is celebrated in its primal entirety.

An activated sacral chakra is the feminine, cozy womb space that holds, nurtures and breeds authentic expression through unconditional love. It is movement and freedom, trust and fierce grace. If it is overactive, you may feel a lack of self-control, emotional instability, distrust and overt sexual addiction, among other things. At the other end of the spectrum, if it is underactive, you may notice you are apathetic toward life, have low self-esteem, fear change, feel restricted or have a very low libido.

Golden topaz

People with bright and balanced second energy centers often stand out in a crowd and bring a sense of magnetic joy to the environment. You have likely spent time or shared space with people who make you feel awesome about yourself. You want to be close to them and are eager to hear what they have to say. They naturally lift you with their contagious confidence, simply through energetic interaction and collaboration. It is almost impossible to maintain a negative mood when in the presence of individuals with healthy sacral chakras – you may even begin to stand taller, smile more and adopt a more positive perspective that, over time, activates your own sacral center.

When you see these people, you know them, because they move with intention, allowing their bodies to take the energetic lead in expressing what is on their minds. As the visionaries of the world, they make it a more artistic place by boldly sharing their creativity for others to learn from and enjoy. Within these individuals comes an incredible gift for union – they are the links that bring people together, whether it be through their art, their interconnectedness with the pulse of the Universe, emotional awareness or their genuine love for others. They are the "creators" among us, impacting their immediate environments and relationships by making them more colorful, loving, sensual and enjoyable.

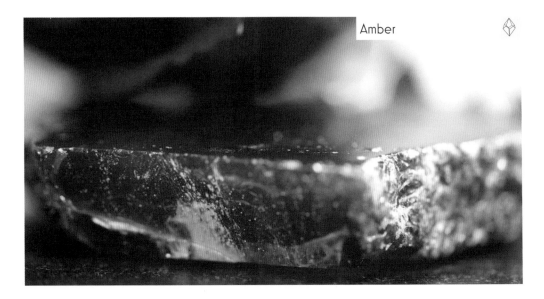

Amber

Of course, the variety of personalities and expressions that exist among this population of sacral vibrant beings is immense. No two people are ever exactly the same, and some of these individuals may be more introverted with smaller friendship circles, enjoying deep and meaningful bonds. Yet, when extroverted, these people can have expansive friendship groups that reach all corners of the earth. They receive energy from discovering new personalities and place themselves in environments that others might deem overwhelming. The common thread uniting these personality types is their desire for purposeful connection and the application of their creative vision in building a fully aligned life, as though it is their masterpiece. They will likely find themselves in friendships and relationships with each other, as well, despite their varying approaches as creators and connectors.

RECLAIMING YOUR SENSUAL SELF

Alongside creativity, the sacral chakra is directly associated with the vitality of the female reproductive organs. Sexuality is the catalyst to reproduction, and reproduction is one of the most incredible forms of human creation. This is the manifestation of intention in its highest form, and it can be applied to other forms of creation as well: sexual energy can be collected, held and diverted to the evolution of ideas, artwork, business, friendship, love and so much more, to birth anything you choose to imagine into present reality. By knowing and acknowledging this boundless power present within all of us, we may overflow with confidence and naturally trust that where we are going, and what we are creating, is of our highest purpose.

Emotional intelligence and wellbeing are attributed to a healthy sacral chakra, and positively contribute to the art of life by making it easier to respond to gut intuition. It is likely you have had a "gut feeling" before, which is a product of the intuitive capabilities inherent within all humans and beings. The second energy center is the origin of your gut feelings. When grounded in the gut, or sacral chakra, the messages provided by this type of intuition are loud, clear and progressively assist you with navigating your best next steps.

However, when the sacral center is muddied and imbalanced, unregulated emotions and responses may make it infinitely more difficult to synthesize the messages of intuition, meaning you are more likely to make emotional decisions that are misaligned with the reality of your situation. The results of this could look like filtering all interactions through a lens of pessimism or distrust, making it difficult to create meaningful connections with others. It could also look like hesitating to take a risk out of fear of failure, and setting limitations on your creativity, goals and dreams. Whichever way it manifests, it is important to remember the value of sensing your intuition before reacting to unchecked emotions. It is better to be led by your inner knowing and be proactive about your life, than to be pulled along by the chaos of assumptions.

Through my work with clients, I discovered that, of all of the chakras, the sacral seems to be one of the most commonly imbalanced energy centers. When I explored histories and past traumas with clients in order to understand the sources of their blockages and ailments, I realized that the number of people who have experienced sexual abuse and shame is quite high. This troubling reality prevents so many individuals from understanding their bodies, sharing their authentic creativity, establishing genuine relationships and feeling free enough to enjoy pleasure. Often, it is as if a thick wall of resistance is erected within their brains, minds and bodies, shutting down the connection and communication between their physical and emotional existence – eventually, their spirit breaks into a thousand little pieces, as a result of living in such numbing dissonance (especially when the default mode is to suppress and ignore, rather than consciously address). Later, we will see how closely linked this energy center is to the fifth energy center (the throat) and how both are impacted by the experiences of the other.

It can be difficult to retrieve each and every piece of somebody's spirit that has been lost when their safety on this earth, and in their bodies, has been deeply jeopardized. It is here that creativity is often shut down. The protective mechanism that occurs in the brain is one that is designed to reduce harm to the psyche; however, when the body and brain dissociate from one another, long after the trauma is over, the impacts can be awful and expand into all areas of life, and chronic illnesses may become more prevalent.

Copper

Other instances that might impact the second energy center include negative thought patterns of feelings of worthlessness, lack of exercise and moments of sexual or creative shame, in which an individual is discouraged from engaging in either art form. A lack of proper sexual education may instill fear around the body and its ability to create life, as well as the changes that occur during puberty. The role that generational behavior plays in this societal pattern is a key issue to highlight here — a single generation must analyze the cycles of shame and choose to be the change that brings about respect and understanding, lest the negative ancestral cycles persist.

When the cycles do persist, the result is generations of people who believe they have no purpose, or are unclear of the direction their lives are meant to go — deep down, their hearts are filled with passion for a path that washed away years ago, and they believe it is too late or impossible to return to their souls' calling. They die with their music still inside them. We also see individuals who are disconnected from their body's knowledge, capabilities and messages, as well as from their emotions. This detachment from the body and emotions generates fear around the body's natural ability to heal, the womb's safety to carry life, the malleability of the mind and brain, and the depth of genuine relationships, further intensifying the chasm that separates them from living a full and vibrant life.

Those who have underactive sacral chakras often find relief in the therapeutic qualities of invigorating dance and movement, which are excellent for awakening this energy center. Overactive sacral chakras also benefit from movement, although they tend to respond well to slow, intentional and sensual practices that warm the body, but do not flood it with overstimulation. For both groups, movement represents an exceptional way to develop an intimate relationship with the body and the emotions stored within it, releasing shadows that have been shut away.

Color can also help. Those with underactive sacral centers benefit from adding orange color accents to their wardrobe and home decor (like crystals, of course). If the client is an artist, I recommend creating artwork with primarily orange hues and displaying these in their homes. The marrying of their artistic expression with creating a harmonious environment enables them to view their art as essential to their sacred space, and removes judgment from their creative process. There is a dramatic shift from creative shame and stagnancy, to abundant flow that leads to creation for the purpose of giving, rather than receiving. Creating to

Honey calcite

130

give allows doubt and hesitation to diminish, because it is less reliant on defining worthiness based on external reassurance. The same applies to sexual self-expression: increasing vital energy through the amplification of orange in one's environment reduces shameful programming and awakens the freedom to step into one's sexuality as a natural, celebratory aspect of the human experience.

Viewing the same process from the perspective of overactivity, I like to cool down the warmth of the sacral chakra with the color blue. So, having a space decorated with combinations of orange and blue strikes a balance in the energetic output from the second center. This helps to stem any leaking energy that is depleting the total life force. If the individual is low in confidence and self-esteem, for example, we might add a little bit of yellow into the equation to bring both the sacral and solar plexus into greater communication. This simple edit has the potential to assist someone who is caught up in the act of expressing for the sole purpose of validation, to honor the worthiness of their energy and direct it to aligned causes.

Orange calcite

SAVORING LIFE

You may be wondering where the physical sense of taste merges with the nature of the sacral chakra; it comes down to two words: *pleasure* and *nourishment*. If what you choose to consume is enjoyable and nurtures your wellbeing, it will carry the same energetic imprint as a balanced second energy center, which primarily deals with pleasure and life-giving creation. On a primal level, the taste sensation gives you the ability to sense whether or not a food is safe to eat, based on how it is perceived by your brain. It also sheds light on what nutrients the food has to offer, depending on if it is sweet, bitter, salty, savory or sour. This process occurs via the gustatory cortex in the frontal lobe, in collaboration with the taste buds. On an emotional level, similar to the smell sensation (these two senses work together, after all), taste can trigger a slew of memories thanks to the insular cortex's connection to the limbic system. By activating the taste sense while holding the illumination statement on page 118 in your brain, you form a positive memory, or association, with that flavor. You can also do this by linking the color orange to the positive emotion. The more that you repeat this practice, the stronger you retrain your brain to initiate a positive emotion in response to it, to the point that you can just imagine the color, or flavor, and energetically embody the illumination.

Obviously, you should never eat a crystal, but there are many ways you can integrate crystals into your dining experience to transform this into an intentional ritual. For example, you can arrange crystals in a grid on the table, taking into consideration the energy you wish to imbue the food with. You might also create an arrangement with flowers and crystals that expresses your creativity and directs the intention of the meal at the same time. Alternatively, you may simply choose to hold a crystal in the palm of your hand during the meal, and infuse your energetic intentions with the essence of the food. In this way, you are not only nourishing the body, but also the mind and spirit as you embrace the illumination mindset and establish a strong association with it through your sense of taste.

Crystals that are orange in color are excellent for sacral chakra healing exercises. Shapes such as roses, portals and *yonis* can carry symbolic significance and contribute to the sensual and creative energy of the sacral chakra. For example, roses serve as reminders to dwell in the warmth and beauty of

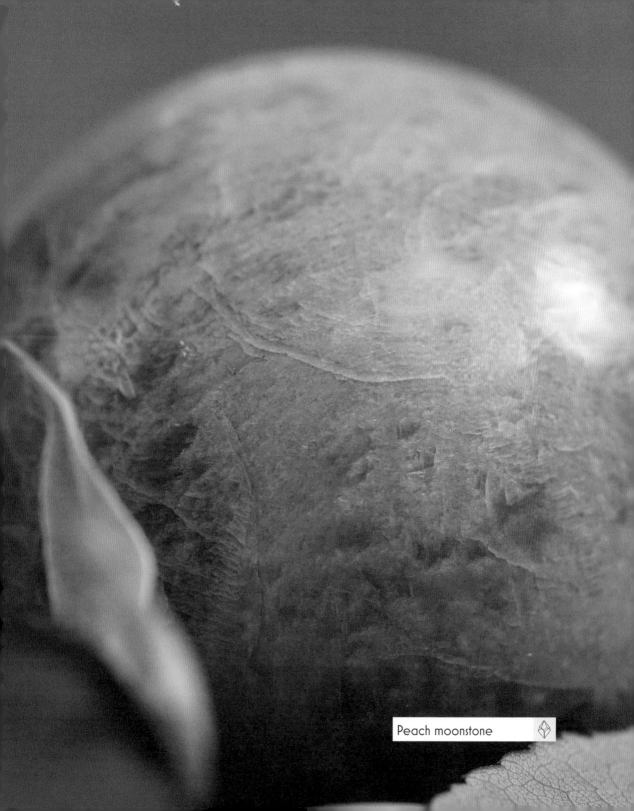

Peach moonstone

Sardonyx

pleasure and creation. Portals are gateways to new dimensions, and encourage exploration into the depths of your creativity – leading to the transmutation of sexual energy into artistic expression, movement or full body presence. *Yoni* is the Sanskrit word for "womb" and the symbol of feminine creation and fertility.

When working with the sacral chakra, it's important to approach the process with wisdom and respect. This energy center holds immense power over your overall wellbeing, and exploring any blockages or imbalances requires sensitivity and understanding. It may be challenging because it can involve opening up after years of closing off. No matter when potential traumas occurred in your life, whether in childhood or later on, it's crucial to treat yourself with gentleness and extend grace to your mind and body. Touching into the vulnerability of the sacral chakra can be an intense experience, so be kind to yourself. Now that you are familiar with how the taste sense, the sacral chakra and the potent energy of creation collaborate in a force of emotion and creation, it is time to experience this energy of creation.

LIQUID GOLD SACRAL SUSTENANCE SOUP

The interplay between crystals, the sacral chakra and the sense of taste opens a gateway to an intimate experience. The following is a simple recipe that makes two servings, which can be used in the meditation that follows.

Ingredients

- 50g/2oz rice
- 200g/7oz ground beef, stewing meat or parboiled beets
- 300g/10½oz diced carrots, fennel and onion
- 1–2 sweet potatoes, diced
- 1 tsp chopped rosemary
- 1 small pinch cayenne pepper
- black pepper, to taste
- 700ml/24fl oz liquid stock

1. Cook the rice according to the packet instructions. While it is cooking, heat the meat or chopped beets in a sauté pan until cooked to your liking. Then add the diced vegetables and sweet potatoes.

2. When the rice is cooked, drain and add to a large pot with the liquid stock, the beef or beets and vegetable medley. Add spices to taste. Cook on low until all flavors blend.

3. Pour into a stone or ceramic bowl and serve in warm lighting.

SACRAL CHAKRA MEDITATION

Prepare your Liquid Gold Sacral Sustenance Soup (or any food that you enjoy which incorporates the color orange). Decorate your surrounding space with sacral chakra crystals, creating a grid or intentional arrangement that imbues your experience with their energies. These crystals will serve as reminders of this experience and encourage connection with the illumination wherever you are. Give yourself time in a quiet space with no distractions and slowly enjoy the soup's flavors. Prepare to begin.

Welcome to your sacral chakra meditation. Shake off the worries of your day . . . the responsibilities of all the things you need to get done. This is your moment. To slow down and become present within your body. To nourish your being with nutrition and gentle self-awareness.

Let your guard down and trust that wherever you are, and wherever you go, you are held and safe to receive. Now, take a deep breath and repeat after me:

I am in Divine flow with the life force energy that birthed the Universe — every expression, emotion and sensation is a reflection of beauty, strength, creativity and creation. I am liquid gold.

With each conscious bite you take, a new flavor and sensation reveals itself to you as it assimilates with the taste buds on your tongue. Eating slowly, you are reminded of the illumination — that you are in Divine flow with the life force energy that birthed the Universe.

Every flavor is a portal to a world where you are comfortable in your body and passionate about your creations. In this world, you are free to be fully embodied in your beauty and sexuality. Without fear of judgment, or being taken advantage of. Your wisdom and expression are received with curiosity and love, by everyone you meet.

Close your eyes now and imagine this place — this experience of complete acceptance and freedom of expression. What does it look like? Maybe it is a field full of colorful, blooming flowers, swaying in the wind with you, as you dance barefoot among their presence. Or perhaps a gentle creek flowing through the canyon, carving orange rock into magnificent shapes. Imagine yourself swaying with the movements of the flowers, or this graceful creek. How does that feel?

Now, sense your hips release and your abdomen relax.

Open your eyes and bring a crystal to your belly, just below your naval . . . hold it there. Continue to enjoy the sustenance of your meal and, as you swallow, envision the nutrients carrying gentle light, and warmth, directly to the location where your hand and crystal meet your sacral energy center, as the food travels through your body. This light radiates outward from your core, filling the rest of you with tingling energy. Every toe and every finger is electric now.

Continue to hold the sensation of pure freedom of creation and expression. You may recall a time in your childhood, or past, where you were discouraged from fully embodying the spirit of your truth, or made to feel unsafe in your body. Forgive the space where you have been holding this memory and release fear, tension and shame. Replace them with joy, creativity and confidence, sending those darker emotions into the crystal to be transmuted into the illumination.

Much like the wildflowers, you are free to bloom — to unapologetically color your environment with your unique magic and light. Your expression and existence make the world a more beautiful place and you deserve to know it — to truly believe it.

Tune in again to the flavors in your mouth for a moment . . . and take a deep breath.

Now again, repeat after me:

I am in Divine flow with the life force energy that birthed the Universe — every expression, emotion and sensation is a reflection of beauty, strength, creativity and creation. I am liquid gold. I am liquid gold. I am liquid gold.

Take this feeling, this memory, with you through the rest of your day or week. Allow it to bring you comfort in your body and send potent energy into your creations; watch how doors open and your life changes.

SOLAR PLEXUS CHAKRA

Key themes:
Confidence, vitality
and abundance

Element:
Fire

Color:
Yellow

Color Psychology:
Cheerfulness, happiness,
brightness, enthusiasm,
comfort, concentration

Sense: Sight

The incredible gift of sight allows
us to analyze the world around
us, visually tune in to the natural
cycles of the Universe and gain
a deeper understanding of the
fractals and patterns that make
up all of life. We get to witness
the magical ways that we, too,
are connected to this beauty!
Whatever it is that you have
access to view in the moment,
do so with deep reverence and
focus, paying attention to how
everything makes you feel.
Whatever is evoked within you is a
message for growth and reflection.

Environment:
A vast desert canyon with the
Sun setting in the distance. The
orange and pink hues of the sky
fill your perception, as the Sun
begins to melt into the sandy red
rocks and mountains ahead. The
warm wind kisses your face, and
the sand beneath your bare feet
draws your consciousness to the
solid earth below you. Shadows
cast over the canyon as the
Sun descends even further and
you breathe in, acknowledging
the incredible force of nature
that is also within you.

Body Awareness:
Upper abdomen, stomach,
liver, gallbladder, pancreas

Subtle Body Auric Layer:
Mental body

SEVEN SOLAR PLEXUS CRYSTALS

The following crystals all support the solar plexus chakra. Think of them as guides to light your way with confidence and joy.

1. Golden Healer quartz
2. Citrine
3. Elmwood calcite
4. Opal
5. Yellow/Sherry topaz
6. Pyrite
7. Sunstone

CITRINE
Optimism

Citrine helps us to see the bright side of life. Even in our darkest moments, we are capable of picturing the silver lining, making us stronger and teaching us lessons that will help us make beneficial, educated decisions that guide us to our greatest success. There is always an opportunity to become better than yesterday, and citrine supports us in manifesting growth and believing in ourselves.

ELMWOOD CALCITE
Clarity

Elmwood calcite infuses the mind with clarity and illumination, providing a beacon of light that guides us toward truth and understanding. By bringing joy and energy through its bright, sunny energy, it disperses the mental fog that causes us to stumble on our path toward progression and abundance. As a result, our journey becomes more enjoyable and easier.

GOLDEN HEALER QUARTZ
Courage

Golden Healer quartz unleashes the fearless warrior within, infusing each of our strides with courage, adventure, boldness and resilience. It motivates us to take action without hesitation, weakening negative thought patterns and replacing them with strategy and purpose. In doing so, Golden Healer quartz brings us closer and closer to our goals while confidently navigating (and appreciating) the present moment.

OPAL
Success

Opal, vibrant in color and energy, channels the integral power of sunlight and strengthens the mind-body-spirit connection, making us stand taller and bringing a sense of knowing that we deserve to achieve our greatest visions and reality. Through this awareness, our visions come to fruition, as we open the portal to our ultimate success.

PYRITE
Abundance

Pyrite is a magnet for abundance and prosperity. With its ability to attract material wealth and abundance, pyrite encourages faith in our ability to manifest the richness of life. It helps us tap into our inner power, unlocking the doors to success, freedom and limitless opportunities. It reminds us that abundance is our birthright and that the Universe is always conspiring to shower us with blessings beyond our wildest dreams.

SUNSTONE
Joy

Sunstone energy is naturally uplifting and hopeful — glittering, sparkling and spreading radiance across all that it comes into contact with. By awakening our playful Inner Child, it reminds us to live life to the fullest and celebrate the simple joys of life that truly matter. Tapping into the fiery energy of sunstone, we approach all of life's challenges with optimism and positivity, overcoming them with the support of joy and happiness.

YELLOW/SHERRY TOPAZ
Confidence

Yellow and Sherry topaz, with hues reminiscent of the Sun's rays, warmly embraces our existence in a hug that empowers us with the confidence to take risks that bring us to the realization of our goals and dreams. With Sherry topaz as our guide, we can rise to new levels of greatness, embodying our most confident versions of self and eradicating doubt.

SOLAR PLEXUS CRYSTAL SUBSTITUTES
Golden apatite, heliodor, lemon quartz, sulphur,
tiger's eye, yellow calcite, yellow jasper

CREATING BALANCE

Crystal(s) in hand, prepare to set your intentions for balancing your solar plexus chakra, and take note of the signs that will show whether you have achieved balance in your third energy center, or whether it remains imbalanced.

MANIFESTATIONS OF BALANCE

Mental	Self-confidence | Motivation | Willpower | Clear decision-making | Inner peace
Physical	High energy levels | Strong metabolism | Healthy skin | Efficient digestion | Proper organ function
Emotional	Maturity and stability | Positivity | Empowerment | Independence | Assertiveness
Spiritual	Potent manifestation | Self-awareness

MANIFESTATIONS OF IMBALANCE

Mental	Perfectionism | Low self-esteem/self-discipline | Indecisiveness | Poor boundaries | Powerlessness
Physical	Constipation or IBS | Adrenal fatigue | Chronic fatigue | Chronic pain | Insomnia
Emotional	Anxiety and/or depression | Irritability | Mood swings | Low stress tolerance | Apathy
Spiritual	No sense of direction | No sense of, or no desire for, purpose

THE SOLAR PLEXUS CHAKRA IS THE CORE

The solar plexus chakra is linked to the color yellow and the Sun. Like the Sun, it helps to keep us in harmony with the natural rhythms of the world. It acts like a conductor, guiding us not only to shine with our brightest light, but also to share our unique strengths confidently with the world. By harnessing the power of our solar plexus chakra, we become empowered to make the world a brighter, healthier and more vibrant place.

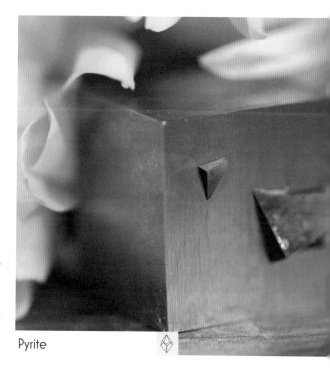

Pyrite

Nestled deep within your ribs and diaphragm, this vibrant hub of energy is responsible for regulating your sense of personal power, confidence and self-worth. It provides you with the strength to stand up for yourself and take on life's challenges.

The wellbeing of the upper abdomen, stomach, liver, gallbladder and pancreas are all associated with the flow quality of this third energy center. When the energy flowing through the solar plexus chakra is optimal, these organs hum with vitality, allowing you to embody your best, most enlivened version of self. Like the pancreas, which plays a vital role in regulating the body's blood sugar levels, the solar plexus chakra is responsible for managing the body's energy levels, acting as a regulator and distributor of the energy throughout the body. So when you focus on balancing and strengthening your solar plexus chakra, you're not just nurturing your spiritual wellbeing — you're supporting your

Citrine

Sherry topaz

physical health in the form of abundant physical and mental energy, glowing skin via nutrient absorption, stable and uplifted moods, and a healthy metabolism.

Nurturing your physical health is key to cultivating a sense of inner strength and confidence. In the case of the solar plexus chakra, you can start by taking steps to support your pancreas, liver and stomach, as well as doing exercises to optimize this energy center. This might involve adopting healthy habits such as eating a well-balanced diet, staying hydrated, exercising regularly and getting enough sleep, while also engaging in confidence-boosting exercises.

STAND TALL

As the core energy center, this chakra is associated with personal power and confidence — the very qualities that help us stand tall and proud. By focusing on strengthening our solar plexus chakra, we can cultivate a strong core and a healthy spine, both physically and metaphorically.

Individuals with a balanced solar plexus chakra tend to exude an air of confidence that is both inspiring and attractive. They possess a deep understanding of their worth and value, and don't feel the need to seek external validation. They have a clear sense of self and are able to assert themselves without being overly aggressive or controlling. Their decision-making skills are top-notch and they're able to navigate life's challenges with ease. Success seems to come to them naturally, as they move through life in a state of true authenticity. These individuals often excel in leadership positions and also flourish in creative or entrepreneurial ventures.

People with a healthy solar plexus chakra not only emanate confidence and personal power themselves, but they encourage those around them to do the same. They do this by embodying qualities such as mutual respect, open communication and genuine encouragement. These individuals radiate an infectious energy that uplifts and inspires those around them. Their bright and sunny personality fills your cup with joy and confidence, as they encourage you to reach your full potential.

Opal

Golden Healer quartz

However, an overactive solar plexus chakra can lead to an individual being overly domineering or stubborn, and unable to see the perspectives of others. They may feel the need to force their will and purpose onto others, driven by a sense of expectation rather than authenticity. In contrast, an underactive solar plexus chakra can result in feelings of insecurity, self-doubt and a lack of confidence in decision-making. These individuals may struggle to assert themselves, often feeling like they need others' approval. They lack a true sense of identity and may drift through life without any clear direction.

Let's take an explorative look at the scenarios where the solar plexus chakra can become unhealthy, imbalanced and dull. Typically, this happens during childhood or adolescence, but it's not uncommon for it to happen at any point in life. It can occur when parents don't support a child's natural talents and inclinations, or when we are forced, as adults, into certain career paths by a particularly domineering authority figure.

There is also another scenario that I see far too often with my clients: individuals in relationships with truly narcissistic people who drain them of energy in order to fulfill their own selfish needs. Over time, the dynamic of these relationships can leave the other person feeling powerless and chemically addicted to the push-and-pull tactics of the person who is draining them. As a result, their identity becomes intertwined with that of the narcissist, wondering what they did wrong or why that person will never truly love them. They begin to seek approval and validation from them, which also seeps into other relationships, and even potential career paths. These individuals often experience symptoms such as constant fatigue, constipation or IBS, a weakened immune system, a fear of rejection or failure, and a lack of purpose and direction in life.

At the other extreme, I encounter clients who struggle with control issues. These individuals have an intense need to maintain control over every aspect of their lives, often due to past experiences where they felt powerless. They may have grown up with narcissistic or authoritarian parents, where any misstep was met with severe consequences and manipulative disappointment, leading to a deep fear of failure. As a result, these individuals may have trouble letting go of control, especially in their romantic relationships. They may feel an overwhelming jealousy when their partner interacts with others, even platonically, and may try to discourage them from developing meaningful relationships with others. But this need for control can have serious consequences for their own health and wellbeing. Those with control issues often experience physical symptoms such as stomach ulcers and acid reflux, as well as emotional symptoms like anger and overactive thoughts that lead to difficulty sleeping. They may also develop rashes or other skin issues as a physical manifestation of their stress and anxiety. Despite these symptoms, letting go of control can be incredibly difficult for them. It requires a great deal of trust and vulnerability, which can be scary for someone who has experienced trauma or feels the need to constantly protect themselves. But with guidance and support, it is possible for these individuals to learn to surrender control, find peace and joy in their relationships, and both share their light and let others shine, too.

TIME TO SHINE

Alongside its connection to the Sun, the solar plexus chakra is linked to the element of fire. Those with an overactive solar plexus can therefore balance their energy by immersing themselves in the color blue. This calming, cool color is associated with water, and helps to bring down the heat of over-aggression. These individuals may seek out blue surroundings, like the sky or a body of water, or incorporate blue crystals such as aquamarine or blue lace agate into their daily life.

For those with an underactive solar plexus, the opposite is true. Surrounding themselves with the color yellow will help to increase the fire energy of the Sun and the solar plexus, thereby boosting personal power and success. Solar plexus crystals like those mentioned earlier are perfect for this purpose, as is anything related to the element of fire, such as lit candles or bonfires.

The solar plexus chakra is intimately tied to the sense of sight as it serves as the gateway to understanding our true identity. When we have a clear vision of who we are, we can truly see all the ways that abundance and success are already within our grasp, and visualize the path to achieving them. Having clear vision is an essential trait for those who exude confidence, self-assurance and a sense of ease in the knowledge that everything they desire is already within their energy field. Not only that, but sight is the very reason why we are able to perceive light from the Sun and view objects within our line of perception. Structures in the eye collaborate to bring in light, which is then directed to the lens to focus on the subject (similar to a camera lens). The light is then transferred to the rods and cones in the retina, to be translated into an electrical impulse that is sent to the occipital lobe in the brain via the optical nerve. And that is how we see. The mind then interprets what it is that we see, in a wonderful waltz between the physical, mental, emotional and spiritual planes.

One powerful exercise that emphasizes the importance of light and sight is sun-gazing. By rising early in the morning and exposing yourself to the red and near-infrared light of the rising Sun within the first 30 minutes of its appearance on the horizon, you can access a multitude of benefits that extend beyond just vision enhancement. This contact with natural light will help to regulate the body's circadian rhythm, enabling it to become attuned to the optimal times for activity

Sunstone

and rest. With healthier skin, better sleep and a longer lifespan all as potential benefits, when practiced safely, sun-gazing is closely related to the solar plexus chakra's mission to increase energy flow and awaken your true potential.

Here is another exercise to help you balance your solar plexus chakra, open your eyes and let the world reveal its majesty to you in new and transformative ways. If you can set up a sacred space somewhere there is an abundance of natural sunlight, I encourage you to bring the Sun into your practice to fill you with its energizing light as you supercharge and balance your third energy center.

Elmwood calcite

THE CRYSTALLINE SOLAR CHARGE

This is a powerful exercise for those who have an underactive solar plexus chakra. By practicing this exercise, you can create a powerful shift in the brain's neural connections that bridges the gap between your current self and the person you want to become.

1. Find a comfortable place to lie down on your back, preferably outside where you can expose yourself to a safe amount of sunlight for about ten minutes. Wear something that bares your solar plexus, to allow the Sun's energy to penetrate directly through the skin.

2. Take a solar plexus crystal — preferably one that is sparkling or translucent to create a play of light and reflection to amplify the Sun's energy — and place it on your diaphragm.

3. Now take long, diaphragmatic breaths in through the nose and exhale deeply through the mouth for about ten breaths.

4. As you breathe, picture who you would be if you were your favorite, most confident and abundant self. Imagine what it would feel like and how you would look, who you would surround yourself with, and what kind of lifestyle you would lead.

5. Know that you are in alignment with your Higher Self and your goals are within reach.

SOLAR PLEXUS MEDITATION

Place a solar plexus crystal (or a picture of one in this book in front of you). Or simply take yourself to a beautiful place where you can sit safely without being disturbed. Wherever you find yourself, I recommend standing for this meditation to encourage a sense of length and confidence in your posture, although you may sit if it is most comfortable for you. Whether sitting or standing, keep your spine and neck long and straight, with your shoulders back and your chest open. Prepare to begin.

Welcome to your solar plexus chakra meditation. Begin by paying close attention to your posture. Is your head weighted forward, or floating perfectly upon your center of gravity? Is your back rounded and chest closed, or are you open and strong? Are you placing more weight on one side of your body than the other, or are you symmetrically aligned? If you find yourself in any of the former positions, consciously choose to shift into the latter.

Now, close your eyes.

Take a very deep breath in through your nose and, as you do, stand or sit up straight, allowing your breath to first fill your diaphragm, then flow into your lungs and open your chest wide. Exhale through your mouth, while maintaining your confident posture.

Take another long, deep breath in through your nose, and exhale out of your mouth. Gently blink your eyes open to gaze upon the object of your interest.

Witness the beauty, colors, shapes and energy that make up this one of a kind, physical expression of a miraculous Universe. What details can you take mental note of as you utilize your sense of sight to soak it in? You might notice textures, ridges, reflections or background details.

What do you see now that you may not have perceived, unless you were truly witnessing it with intention?

Noticing the characteristics that make the subject interesting and unique, imagine yellow sunlight slowly pouring into your space. Everything around you begins to sparkle and shine, and envelops your subject with its energizing, glorious light. As it is filled with golden light, it is activated to radiate its own light outward into the room.

This light approaches you to wrap you in its embrace, gently kissing your skin . . . it starts to tingle. From your toes, to the top of your head, this bubbly sensation travels slowly – lengthening your spine and imbuing you with incredible self-esteem and vibrant confidence.

You might remember a time in your youth when you felt your opinion or aspirations didn't matter. This is your chance to break free from that memory.

Now, a crowd of adoring people appears before you, awaiting the message you have within you to share. You see their smiling faces and sparkling eyes, and you begin to smile, too. Smiling is contagious, after all.

Bring your solar plexus crystal to your diaphragm, where your third energy center resides, and begin to envision it as a disk that is slowly spinning. It spins and spins, progressively picking up speed, until the vibrations of this disk reverberate like waves through your entire body and you become magnetic . . . drawing in abundance, prosperity, and your greatest gifts and intentions. They are all seeking YOU.

Repeat after me:

I am guided and fulfilled by the power of the Sun, drawing in wealth and achievement with my bright spirit and unwavering self-assurance.

The loving crowd erupts in applause and agreement, celebrating your magic and existence.

Focus in again on the subject of your attention; hold the warmth of the light and the energy of the applause in your mind, body and spirit. Remember how it feels to embody your most confident version of self – valued, understood and seen . . . fully capable of achieving your wildest dreams.

Picture exactly what that looks like for you and what it is you want more than anything. Understand that the crowd that cheered you on during this meditation was actually a reflection of your belief in yourself. And go get it!

When you are ready, release your gaze and take this feeling with you through the rest of your day. Witness how your highest intentions become manifest in your world.

SHADOW

"Struggling with a closed and guarded heart, I find it difficult to trust and connect with others, feeling lonely and disconnected even in the midst of relationships."

ILLUMINATION

"With an open and compassionate heart, I attract meaningful connections and abundant love into my life, nurturing and uplifting those around me with ease and grace."

HEART CHAKRA

Key Themes:
Love and relationships

Element:
Air

Color:
Green

Color Psychology:
Harmony, balance, renewal, nature, stability, growth, healing

Sense: Touch

As a species, we're wired to seek out touch, and the more we engage in it – in a mutually caring and respectful way – the more we feel connected and contented. The feel-good hormones of oxytocin and dopamine are released, making us feel happier and closer to others. Even the smallest touch can elevate our mood and restore our sense of wellbeing. By actively seeking out moments of touch and connection in our daily lives, we can nourish our minds, bodies and spirits, and cultivate a greater sense of peace and fulfillment through relationships.

Environment:
A lush, vibrant forest where leaves rustle gently in the breeze. In a peaceful clearing among the trees, with soft, mossy ground underfoot, the element of air flows around you, bringing a sense of lightness and expansion. You feel the softness of the moss beneath you, and the rough bark of the tree behind you as you lean back against it. In this peaceful environment, the heart chakra, the element of air and the sense of touch come together. You immerse yourself in the present moment, feeling a deep connection with the world around you.

Body Awareness:
Lungs, respiratory system, heart, blood, thymus, circulatory system, arms, hands

Subtle Body Auric Layer:
Astral body

SEVEN HEART CHAKRA CRYSTALS

These seven crystals encourage the heart to open with love, embody the illumination and be in harmony with the Universe.

1. Malachite
2. Rhodochrosite
3. Rose quartz
4. Kunzite
5. Epidote
6. Dioptase
7. Vivianite

DIOPTASE
Compassion

Dioptase encourages us to deepen our understanding of others and to extend kindness to them, even (and especially) when we do not understand their actions. Everyone is walking a path we know nothing about, and approaching others with non-judgment can create a more loving environment for all. This Divine Feminine approach to relationships makes the world a better place, one person at a time.

EPIDOTE
Heart-centeredness

Epidote inspires us to create a life filled with purpose and meaning. It guides us to make decisions and connections that align with our heart's desires, leading to a more authentic and fulfilling existence. When we live from a heart-centered space, we attract people, experiences and opportunities that are in harmony with our true selves, creating a sense of synchronicity and wonder in our lives.

KUNZITE
Self-love

Kunzite is a powerful ally on the journey toward self-love. By embracing all aspects of ourselves, even those considered to be less desirable, we can truly begin to accept and love who we are. This integration of our light and shadow aspects helps to heal old wounds, allowing us to attract relationships that match the level of self-love we have cultivated.

MALACHITE
Evolution

Malachite is a catalyst for heart evolution, awakening the potential for deep and transformative growth. It breaks down old patterns and beliefs that once limited the ability to love, or to accept oneself and others. As the heart expands, a sense of renewal emerges, inspiring us to step into a version of self that is brimming with the confidence and radiance needed to attract beautiful connections and relationships.

RHODOCHROSITE
Healthy emotion

Rhodochrosite encourages healthy emotional expression, helping to release and heal past traumas that create blockages in the heart and hinder emotional growth. Through this process we get better at communicating our emotions and, thus, strengthen our relationships with our honesty and transparency. By improving our emotional awareness and acceptance, we navigate life with more ease, cultivating fulfilling relationships and experiences.

ROSE QUARTZ
Unconditional love

Rose quartz eases the pain and emotional wounds that shut us off from receiving the abundance of love that surrounds us. When we hurt, it is much more challenging to accept love and, therefore, to give love. This crystal's gentle energy comforts us, helping us face our fears and insecurities around love with grace. By using rose quartz, we gain a deeper understanding of ourselves and others, building meaningful connections based on unconditional love.

VIVIANITE
Harmony

Vivianite engages us with the rhythm of the Universe, enabling us to form a profound understanding of who we truly are in relation to the world around us. It inspires trust that we may develop harmonious relationships with others and cultivate more self-love, without fear of getting hurt in the process. It reminds us that the past is the past, and releases negative emotional blockages that prevent us from achieving inner peace and serenity through love.

HEART CRYSTAL SUBSTITUTES
Chrysoprase, fuchsite, green tourmaline, morganite, prehnite, rhodonite, seraphinite

CREATING BALANCE

Once you've selected a heart crystal or two and set your intentions for balancing this energy center, here are the signs that will show whether you have achieved balance, or whether it remains imbalanced.

MANIFESTATIONS OF BALANCE

Mental	Clear identity | Open-mindedness | Emotional intelligence | Empathy | Genuine
Physical	Strong heart | Healthy blood pressure | Good circulation | Deep, clear breathing | Good posture
Emotional	Love and compassion | Security and trust | Deep relationships | Forgiveness | Generosity
Spiritual	Receptivity to the world | Sense of oneness

MANIFESTATIONS OF BALANCE

Mental	Inability to express | Difficulty connecting | Negative self-talk | Lack of emotional regulation | Inability to trust
Physical	Heart palpitations | Asthma and/or other respiratory issues | Chest pain | High blood pressure | Cold hands or feet
Emotional	Jealousy | Resentment | Need for reassurance | No self-love | Fear of intimacy/detachment
Spiritual	Isolated from outside connections | Selfish tendency to focus solely on self

THE HEART CHAKRA IS THE VITAL BEAT

Located at the center of the chest, right beside the actual heart and within the sternum, lies the heart chakra. It's the energy center that radiates the very essence of who you are. Just as love is the life force of humanity, connecting us and enabling us to thrive, so is the heart chakra the vital beat that sustains our energetic existence. It's the core of our being, and the compass that guides us in our relationships with the world and with others. This amazing energy center attracts positivity and abundance through its powerful electromagnetic field. When this fourth energy center is balanced and thriving, we experience a fulfilling heart-centered life, overflowing with meaningful connections that light up our lives.

If we nurture and activate our heart chakra in our daily lives, we open ourselves up to a whole new level of understanding and compassion. We're able to approach the world with a sense of reverence and peace, attracting only the very best people and experiences, and creating a magnetic force that attracts all that is good and pure. The fourth primary chakra is responsible for our ability to connect deeply with others, nurture quality relationships, extend compassion and forgiveness, and experience genuine, vulnerable love. It's a center-point for wellness in all of our energy centers, sitting right in between the three lower chakras and the three upper ones.

Malachite

Not only is this energy center directly linked to the physical heart, it is also connected to the thymus gland, the lungs and the circulatory system. These body

Vivianite

parts either directly work with, or are correlated to, the flow of blood and oxygen throughout the body. Think of oxygen and blood as the two essential life force elements of the physical body, much like the heart chakra is the life force of our spiritual existence. When everything is working in harmony and alignment, the quality of our lives and happiness soars, and our overall wellbeing is strengthened by the life-giving nature of breath, air and blood. We have meaningful relationships, explore intimacy with open minds and hearts, and can more easily move past unhealthy grudges, among many other things.

Let's take a closer look at the connection between the heart chakra and the thymus gland, which plays a crucial role in supporting the body's immune system. Located in the front part of the chest, just behind the sternum, the thymus gland is responsible for the development of T-cells, which are essential in fighting off infections and diseases. It is also responsible for producing hormones known as thymosins, which stimulate the maturation of the T-cells, which then go on through the bloodstream to find foreign bodies such as viruses, bacteria and even cancer cells to fight. The heart chakra and the thymus gland are situated almost exactly next to each other within the chest bone, at the center of our emotional and energetic connections to the world around us. When our heart chakra is in balance, it not only keeps us energetically healthy, but can support our immune system in its fight against disease.

This powerful energy center also modulates the impact of the energies we encounter from others in our environment, helping us navigate the ups and downs of daily life with grace and ease. So, just as we nourish our bodies to keep our immune system strong, we must also nourish our heart chakra to keep our emotional and energetic connections healthy and balanced. After all, it's all part of the interconnected system that keeps us alive and thriving.

A healthy heart chakra naturally seeks out others with a similar energy, creating a beautiful, magnetic bond between two people. Those with a balanced fourth energy center tend to lead with their chest and stand tall, exuding a sense of openness and trust. When we present ourselves in this way, we become more approachable and inviting, making it easier for other warm-hearted individuals to enter our world. The opposite is also true. Individuals who hunch their shoulders and round their back may be signaling a lack of trust and a desire to protect their heart. Though we do not need to consciously pay attention to who is leading with their chest, and thus their heart, because it is in our nature to sense this subconsciously. We can intentionally look for new connections with those who match the energetic frequency of love, openness and empathy based on the physical ways in which they carry themselves. Are they leading with their chest, or are they protecting themselves? By paying attention to these subtle cues, you may be able to better understand the energy they bring to the table, and whether or not it's a good match for you.

Dioptase

CONNECTING FROM THE HEART

If you have met someone with a vibrant heart chakra, you may have sensed the way that their gentle nature radiates out from their heart like an electromagnetic field. Being near them can have a palpable effect, as their ability to sync other people's heart rates with their own can create a physiological connection that you may not consciously realize, but you can certainly feel.

These people are incredibly empathetic and live in a state of non-judgment because they understand where others are coming from. Giving and receiving love comes naturally to them, and their very presence can make you feel incredibly warm and at ease. These characteristics make them perfect for roles in which they are caretakers or support a cause they are passionate about, because their empathy drives them to care so deeply about what they do. They are also incredible artists due to their amazing ability to express their emotions. These individuals often live in joy because they are capable of experiencing a deep sense of gratitude that helps them to appreciate their life. In short, people with balanced heart chakras are true gems, shining bright with love and compassion for themselves and the world around them. Because of this, they make it easier for other people to be vulnerable enough to do the same.

People with balanced heart chakras are like a breath of fresh air in relationships, whether those are romantic or platonic. With their exceptional communication skills, they have a way of establishing deep connections with those they love. They are easy to have productive conversations with, and always seek to understand and resolve conflicts in a constructive manner. They listen intently to the needs and desires of others while effectively communicating their own, resulting in a nurturing and open exchange that strengthens the foundation of their relationships. Being in a relationship with these individuals feels like being unconditionally cherished and truly seen. It is no wonder that they have such meaningful and fulfilling relationships with those around them. Even if they are no longer a part of your world, they can leave you a better person because of their influence on your existence.

TRUSTING TO LOVE

Let's explore some common experiences that can throw this delicate energy center out of balance, based on my experience working with clients. When imbalance does strike the heart chakra, the effects can be intense and detrimental in a variety of ways.

Betrayal is one of the quickest ways to upset the heart chakra. Whether it's discovering a long-hidden secret or being cheated on by a significant other, betrayal can shatter the trust that is crucial for keeping our hearts open and healthy, and lead to an underactive fourth energy center. After a betrayal, it's hard to believe that relationships can be safe and loving spaces when someone you thought you knew so well turns out to be someone completely different. In fact, this kind of emotional pain can make it challenging to ever love again. Those with underactive heart chakras tend to be emotionally numb and disconnected from others. They may struggle to feel deep love or compassion, and the lack of relational fulfillment and intimacy can lead to depression,

Epidote

as we humans are inherently social creatures who thrive in community. On a physical level, low blood pressure, circulation problems like cold hands and feet, and heart disease can all be manifestations of this imbalance.

An underactive heart chakra can also stem from the loss of a loved one. It could be the death of a cherished family member, a miscarriage or even the trauma of watching a parent leave the home due to divorce. It's as though a steel wall is erected around the heart to protect these individuals from the intense grief and pain that comes with losing someone they love. Unfortunately, this wall can become a prison, trapping them in a cycle of emotional deflection and isolation. It's a protective mechanism that shields them from the pervasive heartbreak of loss, but it also prevents them from experiencing love and connection in the future — a repeating cycle that must be halted and rerouted into more empowering and productive habits and behaviors.

Kunzite

The fear of losing someone we love can be overwhelming, making it easier to avoid love altogether, because that experience is too difficult to imagine facing again and again. But with time, self-compassion and heart chakra healing exercises, these individuals can begin to dismantle that wall and restore balance to this energy center. They can learn to honor their loss as a pivotal moment of awareness and growth, while also opening themselves up to the possibility of sacred union and relationship once more.

Another scenario that can upset the heart chakra is emotional neglect in childhood. When a child's caretakers are cold, distant and inattentive to their needs, this can have long-lasting effects on their ability to form healthy relationships. Children naturally seek out warmth and safety from their parents, so when they don't receive this critical part of their development, they may grow up feeling desperate for love and attention, or become hyper-independent and closed off to love altogether. It's a sad outcome either way, and when it happens early in life, it can take a lot more time and work to bring these individuals back to a state of heart homoeostasis. Young children do not have the tools and understanding to process a lack of love — a love that would have enabled them to develop a secure attachment style, and which would have translated into feelings of trust, confidence and safety later on in their own adult relationships.

At the opposite end of the spectrum, I've found that children who had to bear the weight of their parents' emotional baggage from a young age may end up with overactive heart chakras. This can manifest in a few ways, sometimes caused by parents who fight and put their children in the middle of their conflicts by venting and gossiping, or who require their children to do the emotional labor they are not yet equipped to handle. For these children, it can seem like this is just what love looks like, and they may believe that their ability to listen and be there for their parents is what makes them a "good" child. In fact, their identity may become wrapped up in their listening skills, because it's the only form of focused attention they receive from their stressed and unhappy parents.

Unfortunately, when these children grow up, they often become desperate for love and connection with others, even if those relationships are not healthy or mutually beneficial. When suffering from a fear of abandonment that drives them to seek closeness with others at any cost, they may attract partners who mimic the rocky relationships they witnessed growing up. To them, any love is better than no love at all, even if it means repeatedly falling into bad relationships that are simply repeated patterns of what they learned love looks like growing up.

For those with overactive heart chakras, jealousy and possessiveness tend to arise, and they often struggle with setting healthy boundaries. If they do try to set boundaries, they may not know how to implement them effectively, leading to a tendency to take on too much, or sacrifice themselves for others. On the physical plane, chest pain, heart palpitations and high blood pressure can all be caused by the excess energy coursing through the heart center. It's like a traffic jam on the highway, but instead of cars, it's energy that is causing a slew of problems.

It's clear that balance is key when it comes to the heart chakra. Finding the sweet spot where emotions are felt but are not overwhelming, and where love and compassion are abundant but not stifling, will keep your heart center spinning harmoniously. So, just how can those with imbalanced heart chakras find their way back to a place of love, trust and connection? It can be a challenging journey that takes courage and patience, but there are practices to assist with shifting into new perspectives and behaviors, and the rewards are worth it — a heart that is open, vibrant and ready to experience all that life has to offer.

You can utilize color therapy in conjunction with the elements to assist in your path back to a balanced fourth energy center. The heart chakra is linked to air, so when it is overactive, the color red becomes an ally. By immersing yourself in the grounding and stabilizing properties of red, you can step entirely into your body and release the heavy emotions that are holding you back. But be conscious of not overdoing it — too much red can raise your blood pressure and exacerbate an already overactive heart. Instead of turning your bedroom into a kingdom of red sheets and wall art, try incorporating red quartz or smokey quartz crystals into your daily routine, and seek out natural environments where you can connect with the Earth and ground yourself.

For those with underactive heart chakras, the color green can help to increase vibrational energy and promote the qualities of air that sustain all living things. Heart chakra crystals are ideal for this purpose, and by using the power of color and the balance of elements, you can find yourself in a state of heart-centered equilibrium once again. In one simple yet effective exercise, I encourage my clients to imagine a beautiful green ball of light forming in the center of their chest, in the area of their heart center. With each deep breath they take, the green light grows bigger and brighter, filling every nook and cranny of their body before spilling out into the environment around them. Next, I ask them to visualize the people they have lost, those who may have caused them to shut off from giving, or receiving, love. They imagine these people standing in the room with them, surrounded by the potent, warm and loving energy of the green light. As the light grows even bigger and begins to exit the room, it floats freely throughout the outside world, enveloping everything and everyone it touches with the energy of compassion and open-heartedness. (We'll be drawing on a similar approach in the meditation at the end of this chapter.)

Touch is another important aspect of the heart chakra. It is one of the first senses that a fetus develops in the early weeks of pregnancy. As humans, we crave touch from the moment we are born, and it continues to be a vital aspect of our lives as we grow older. Thanks to the somatosensory system, our entire bodies are covered inside and out by sensory receptors that send electrical pulses from neuron to neuron, to be relayed by the spinal cord to the brain to be processed. How we perceive touch determines our reaction to it — touch can be too aggressive and hard, or make us feel safe and nurtured. Touch can also become an aspect of loss, as it can be painful when we no longer have the opportunity to connect physically with someone in the way we once did. Through intentional touch exercises, such as heart-to-heart hugging, we can still experience the benefits of physical connection and build relationships that are fulfilling and meaningful.

Use touch to tap into your tactile senses with crystals, too, by holding a heart chakra crystal or placing it on part of your body, and tuning in to its temperature and texture.

Rose quartz

Run your fingers across its surface and feel the edges as you close your eyes, creating a deep connection between your brain and the sensation. With each crystal, you'll embark on a new adventure, exploring its contours and connecting with its essence in a profound way. By being intentional about how we engage in touch and by recognizing the power it has in our lives, we can create meaningful connections with others and experience the benefits of touch for ourselves.

Now that we have delved into the intricacies of the heart chakra, prepare yourself for a hands-on experience in which we will combine the energy of heart chakra crystals and the sense of touch to activate your heart, increase love in your life, and release any heartbreak or grief that has been keeping you from moving forward. We'll also work on forgiving the grudges that have been weighing heavily on your heart and draining your energy. Gather your crystals and find a peaceful, comfortable and safe space to connect with yourself and your heart. It's time to let unconditional love flow in.

Rhodochrosite

GLOW WITH GRATITUDE

A gratitude practice is very effective for balancing an overactive heart chakra. This simple yet powerful exercise creates feelings of love and reassurance, showing the brain that it is safe to let go and that love can exist without having to hold on too tightly.

1. In your Gem Sorcery journal, create a list of people and things you are grateful for in your life.

2. As you read through the list, note down any fears you may have around abandonment, jealousy or possessiveness. By bringing these feelings to the conscious mind, you can begin to understand why they are there and whether they serve a positive purpose.

3. Next, consider where these emotions are held in the body and what they look like. Often, you will recognize that these negative feelings are eating away at your wellbeing.

4. To reinforce this newfound understanding, you can write down a few characteristics you love about each person on your gratitude list.

5. Then, state out loud that you release them to continue evolving into the beautiful beings they are and will be.

6. Finally, I encourage you to send a message to (or call) these individuals, to let them know you love and care about them, without any expectations or strings attached.

HEART CHAKRA MEDITATION

Create a cuddle puddle with your softest pillows, blankets
and comforting items that feel lovely to the touch. Consider
meditating with a partner, holding hands to connect their skin
to yours. Gather your favorite heart chakra crystals and explore
their sensations against your body. Prepare to begin.

*Welcome to your heart chakra meditation. Loving spirit, now is the moment
to create space for your heart's healing, by lying on your back and draping
yourself in a soft, cozy blanket. Ensure that your environment is peaceful and
quiet, allowing you to tune in to the sound of your own heartbeat and breath.*

*Your legs should extend out beneath you, with your feet relaxed
underneath the blanket. Notice how it rests upon the skin of
your toes . . . then, your shins . . . your knees and thighs . . . and
then, your hips . . . everywhere the blanket makes contact with
your body, bring your awareness to the sensation of touch.*

*Hold a heart chakra crystal in the palm of each hand, facing them up
to the sky. You notice the weight of the crystals in the palms of your
hand and the weight of your back against the floor. Allow yourself to
sink into the ground and truly let down your guard. You are safe here.*

*Bring your consciousness to your breath now. Feel how your heart beats
gently within your chest, as it rises up and down with each breath . . . in
and out. Take one long deep breath in, filling your lungs and diaphragm
to ultimate capacity and then release with a loud sigh, exhaling from your
mouth. In this moment, your jaw falls into a relaxed position — keep it there.
Close your eyes and prepare to be transported to another place and time.*

*On the ground around you, green moss is slowly beginning to form. The air
becomes moist, making your skin slightly dewy, and you begin to hear calls
from the birds of rainforests. Suddenly, you arrive in a thick forest full of trees
and plants of all kinds towering over you. Everything is sparkling from a*

fresh rainfall; there are no other humans around, just the majestic creatures of the forest. Pay attention to the temperature of the air . . . pleasantly mild.

Bring your hands with the crystals to your chest and make contact with your heart. Picture everyone you love, and have ever loved . . . they are present with you and their energies felt. Someone you love. Someone you lost. Someone you don't speak to anymore. Someone you trust. Whoever these people may be . . . send them your love and compassion in the form of a radiant green, glowing light. Emanating out from your heart, the green light envelops each individual in its energy.

Extend forgiveness to the individuals that hurt you, who stifled your innocence and led your Inner Child not to trust.. Their pain is no longer yours to carry and the weight of that darkness breaks free, then merges to become one with the Earth – transmuted into new life. Flowers sprout and bloom where that pain used to be.

With your hands still on your beating heart and the crystals making contact with your chest, take a deep breath, sending this directly into your palms. Exhale and repeat:

With an open and compassionate heart, I attract meaningful connections and abundant love into my life, nurturing and uplifting those around me with ease and grace.

As you finish your last sentence, the forest and all the people you love slowly begin to fade, carrying the loving energy of that green light with them to hold onto forever.

As you open your eyes, you bring your awareness to the room, where a soft green hue continues to fade until you are fully in your body and consciousness again.

You are present in your heart center. Continue to lead from this space and connect in new, fulfilling ways.

SHADOW

"I am unable to manifest the energy of my mind and thoughts into reality, using the sound waves of my voice. My words do not matter, or make an impact, so I keep my truth inside."

ILLUMINATION

"I speak confidently and clearly, with dedication to my truth and authenticity. By doing so, I honor and uplift those for whom my message is an asset."

THROAT CHAKRA

Key Themes:
Communication, self-expression and connection

Element:
Ether

Color:
Blue

Color Psychology:
Wisdom, serenity, authority, confidence, trust, peace, dependability, loyalty

Sense: Hearing

Sounds help us to make sense of the world and communicate our place in it. When our mind is hyperactive, or juggling the recurring stresses of our daily lives, we may miss the opportunity to assess how the surrounding sounds make us feel on a subconscious level. When we slow down and truly listen, we will hear the background music of our life. Pause and listen to nature, to the workings of our body and to music. Ask, "Do these sounds cause me distress? Does this music empower me? Do I feel more peaceful?" Addressing these questions will turn off our auto-pilot and establish a state of awareness.

Environment:
A wide open space of green grass, or a field of flowers, on a sunny day. A soft blanket covers the ground beneath your back, as you lie and look up at the bright blue sky. Fluffy, billowy clouds are drifting by, covering the Sun just enough to witness its golden rays pouring out like honey from behind them. The rays appear as though they are a portal to the ether – the heavens.

Body Awareness:
Throat organs, tongue, jaw, thyroid, parathyroid, neck/cervical spine, shoulders

Subtle Body Auric Layer:
Etheric template

SEVEN
THROAT CHAKRA
CRYSTALS

These seven crystals can cut through the clatter and chatter of daily life, and open the gateway to deep connections and communications through embodying the energy of the illumination.

1. Chrysocolla
2. Blue lace agate
3. Sodalite
4. Teal fluorite
5. Blue chalcedony
6. Blue kyanite
7. Lapis lazuli

BLUE CHALCEDONY
Reflection and presence
Blue chalcedony puts a pause on the hustle and bustle of societal norms, and slows down repetitive thoughts and tasks, so we can be more intentional in how we approach life. With its often glossy appearance and subtle blue coloration, this stone reminds us to reflect on our path and choose a life of embodied presence. In doing so, we express our truth eloquently and clearly in a manner that is effective and efficient.

BLUE KYANITE
Authenticity
Blue kyanite amplifies courage in all realms of communication and excites the energy of authenticity to rise from the deepest spaces of our mind, body and spirit. With this blue stone in hand, we become less self-conscious of how others may perceive us through their own lens of experience, and become the most vibrant version of our true self by shedding the layers behind which we may be hiding.

BLUE LACE AGATE
Mental peace
Blue lace agate offers the opportunity to silence the noise of doubt, anxiety and fear, which undermine our mental peace and drain our energy. Its characteristic soft blue hue signals to our brain a calming atmosphere of angelic energy, allowing our thoughts and perception to begin to match the vibrational frequency of tranquility and peace.

CHRYSOCOLLA
Honesty
Chrysocolla is a natural bridge between the heart and the throat, which opens up a line of communication that enables our emotions to be transformed into externalized truth. The heart chakra is perpetually honest about what it feels and what it truly desires. By bringing the messages of the heart into the vocal space of the throat chakra, chrysocolla brings honesty to expression.

LAPIS LAZULI
Wisdom

Lapis lazuli links to the throat and third eye, opening a portal of inner wisdom and intuition that guides the development of impactful communication. The resulting knowledge serves as the source for an overflowing well of information that has the power to uplift our communities and positively change the world, as we share our wisdom.

SODALITE
Communication

Sodalite bears the ultimate crown of exquisite communication, influencing how we choose to speak and how confidently we do so. It brings an ease to our words and a sophisticated flow in our ability to connect with whomever we speak with, thereby establishing the important foundations for understanding and collaboration.

TEAL FLUORITE
Clarity

Teal fluorite establishes lucidity and clears fog from the process of thought. In turn, greater levels of clarity and understanding are achievable, bringing ease to the formation of genuine insight and expression of our truth. Our mind is the mirror and teal fluorite is the holistic cleaning agent that distills the mind's reflections.

THROAT CRYSTAL SUBSTITUTES

Amazonite, aquamarine, angelite, blue apatite, blue aventurine, blue calcite, celestite

CREATING BALANCE

Once you've chosen your throat crystal(s) and set your intentions for balancing this chakra, certain signs will show whether you have achieved balance, or whether your fifth energy center remains imbalanced.

MANIFESTATIONS OF BALANCE

Mental	Innovation | Leadership | Authenticity | Creativity | Communication
Physical	Clear, smooth voice | Good hearing | Strong breathing | Regulated metabolism | Energetic
Emotional	Receptive | Pride | Confidence | Honesty | Self-assurance
Spiritual	Sense of self-value | Personal freedom

MANIFESTATIONS OF BALANCE

Mental	Timid | Detachment | Righteousness | Gossip | Argumentative
Physical	Sore throat | Tooth or jaw pain | Upper back discomfort and/or scoliosis | Thyroid dysfunction | Headache
Emotional	Inadequacy | Insecurity | Suspicion | Nerves | Shame
Spiritual	Lack of purpose | No sense of boundaries

THE THROAT CHAKRA IS THE GREAT CONNECTOR

Your voice is one of the most powerful tools you possess. This is because all language carries a vibration, which ultimately attracts the equivalent physical expression of that vibration. Simply put, the energy behind what you say, and how you say it, shows up in your quality of life. How you choose to express yourself and your ideas affect the environment in which you build your community. Therefore, being purposeful with your words and speaking in alignment with your truth will strengthen your message and enhance your outcomes. We all know the saying that misery loves company, but so do honesty and positivity. When you understand this and embody the illumination on page 176, you will lay a firm foundation for developing a healthy, activated and balanced throat chakra – because having conscious awareness of your voice's influence on reality truly is a superpower.

Considering that our throat houses our vocal cords and the muscles in charge of speech, it is obvious why the throat chakra governs communication and self-expression. The throat chakra is located directly between the heart and third eye chakras, and is represented by the color blue. Not only is it associated with the throat organs and thyroid gland, but also the neck, shoulders, mouth, jaw, upper back and ears.

The fifth energy center is located in an area of the body that joins the lower, earthly chakras with the highest chakras, an area that can be prone to energetic "bottlenecks" (notice how the word "neck" is in there?), depending on the efficiency through which

Blue kyanite

information flows to, and from, its location. A blockage is akin to heavy traffic being funneled from a four-lane highway into a two-lane highway. With nowhere to go, the traffic – or in this instance, the energy – builds up and stagnates. The electrical potential of the body gets impacted and experiences physical repercussions like chronic neck and back pain, sore throats and jaw tension. To add to that, body language closes off, posture becomes poor, frustration builds and sense of purpose diminishes. Like every driver on the road, each chakra takes a hit as a result of the bottleneck up ahead.

Blue chalcedony

As the "Great Connector" of the lower and higher chakras, the health of the throat has significant capacity for life-changing mental, physical, emotional and spiritual effects. The thyroid, one of the most important glands in the endocrine system, is located in this energy center and deals with the production of energy that fuels vital bodily functions, such as breathing and circulating blood. Thyroid hormones significantly influence ATP production in the mitochondria, which is one source of the body's cellular energy levels. If energy is lacking or overabundant, then balance is challenging to achieve and all the dominoes may begin to fall. Additionally, ATP plays a role in the functions of the muscular system, cardiac system, the transfer of information from neuron to neuron and more. It also plays an important part in fertility and menstruation, with the latter being called the "fifth vital sign" of women's wellbeing. If menstruation is nonexistent, for example, and this isn't due to menopause, it may be a warning signal that something is going wrong within the body's biological functions and a larger issue needs to be addressed.

Taking conscious care and action to nurture this energy center is vital to both the physical and spiritual flow of energy throughout the body. In other words, how you choose to express yourself correlates with how well the body communicates between the different parts of itself; however, it will always be very clear about expressing when something is not right, even when you are not. Pay attention to its messages and listen intently — the ability to do so is another sign of a balanced throat chakra.

SPEAKING YOUR TRUTH

When you have the courage to express yourself authentically and honestly, without fear of ridicule, and have the capacity to listen intently to other points of view, you likely have a vibrant, balanced throat chakra. A healthy throat chakra is also indicated by strong creativity, due to clarity of perspective and potent connection to your source of emotional expression.

Individuals with bright and healthy fifth energy centers tend to be natural leaders, with a very clear vision of their purpose and what they are here to accomplish in this lifetime. These people effortlessly magnetize support for their mission because they are not forceful in their perspectives or methods for achieving goals — they trust that what is meant for them will unfold in magical ways. It is already theirs, and thus, there is no stress or anxiety surrounding the materialization of said purpose. With direction and confidence, a leader efficiently influences their supporters to care about their goal with equal passion, building an energetic and intentional armory to send into the field; failure seems near impossible at this level of people-power and flow, and it is only a matter of time before success is realized.

A person with a balanced throat chakra may not always choose to be a leader, of course. The ability to speak one's truth with eloquence and tap into full, conscious expression is applicable in all realms of life. Not only does this energy center have the power to establish strong relationships built on mutual respect, it also makes it easier to receive what is desired, as a result of having the ability to ask for it. How this manifests is very individual, depending on each person's level of introversion or extroversion, but simply having the confidence to vocalize an idea or need opens the door to opportunity — in work, love, friendship, adventure and experience. As the old saying goes, "the squeaky wheel gets the grease."

However, an overactive throat chakra might be indicated by gossiping, speaking off the cuff without first being thoughtful of what we share, lying and having weak listening skills. Alternatively, if you are hesitant to speak up in groups, or to stand in your authenticity, your throat chakra may be underactive and imbalanced. You may find it difficult to speak clearly, or project your voice, and you allow people to continuously speak over you in group settings.

Various experiences can affect the overall wellness of your fifth energy center, and harm your ability to communicate and express yourself in a healthy way. For example, we have likely all encountered at least one person who has embarrassed us by shooting down an idea of ours, or judged us for what we are wearing. A one-off incident may or may not have a lifelong impact, but if the criticism continues, we might begin to question whether it is safe to share such vulnerable and authentic parts of ourselves. We then begin to shape ourselves according to the perceived expectations and desires of those around us, rather than what makes us unique and whole. In another example, we may find ourselves in a relationship where it is not safe to speak up, and our perspectives are not valued, so we either shut down entirely because it takes up too much energy to attempt to be heard, or we develop a deep anger that fuels every future interaction that involves getting our thoughts across. At these levels of repression and forcefulness, respectively, there is a disconnect that occurs where energy is either not flowing enough as a result of our being too self-conscious, or burning off too quickly through heavy and unconscious release.

In my work, I have discovered that a repressed throat chakra may often be caused by experiences of sexual and physical abuse, when someone has felt unable to find or use their voice to successfully speak out. Oftentimes, the mind dissociates from the experience in order to protect itself and everything becomes muted; thoughts and emotions get separated from conscious awareness. This protective mechanism is triggered with each traumatic experience, until it sets in as a continuous pattern. Following traumatic experiences, it can be even harder to open up and share what occurred, whether it be out of the fear of not being believed or of "rocking the boat," which in turn worsens the blockage in the throat chakra. These people tend to experience a sense of apathy and lose touch with the Divine Source that they are a part of (which makes complete sense given the fact that the fifth energy center is, again, the gateway to the third eye and crown chakras). Other common symptoms I see are tense shoulders that drift up toward the ears, hunched posture, chronic back pain, busy tongues, clenched jaws and a hyperactive thyroid as the body tries to compensate for the imbalance. All that pent-up energy has to go somewhere.

At the other end of the spectrum, I have worked with clients who did not feel seen or heard in childhood, who were not supported or were bullied, and now often feel the need to overcompensate in adulthood in order to prove themselves. Their sense of self is highly dictated by how the world perceives them, which sometimes leads to aggressive behavior and a tendency to lie in order to feel more valuable. This is another protective mechanism because its primary goal is for the individual to remain safe and comfortable; however, it is only a matter of time before such behavior begins to hurt a person's relationships, opportunities and their overall quality of life. These

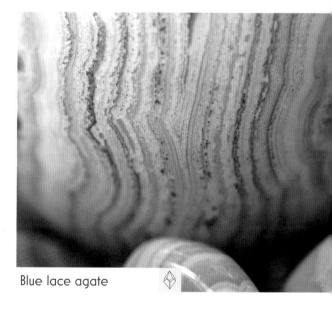

Blue lace agate

people tend to feel alone in the world and to undermine their own opportunities for success because, on a subconscious level, they feel undeserving of the good things in life, or do not trust that other people have good intentions for them. They tend not to think about how other people feel or analyze other people's perspectives, because their goal is to keep themselves safe from any potential criticism that could shake up their entire identity.

Chrysocolla

Symptoms that I witness in these clients are headaches, an underactive thyroid, fatigue and tooth ache, although presentations vary from person to person. They expend so much energy into the external world, or spend so much time worrying, that there is not enough energy for the physical body to utilize, which leads to sluggishness.

RESTORING HARMONY

Depending on the presentation of imbalance in the throat chakra, a client may benefit from vocal exercises that open the throat and empower the voice. Singing, humming, sighing and even screaming are excellent for shaking off stagnant energy and lengthening tense vocal cords. However, those clients with overactive throat chakras may benefit from taking time out during the day to meditate and sit in pure silence, to avoid activation of the vocal cords. Again, this is because overuse leads to exhaustion. In order to recuperate their energy, it is important to reel it in.

Intentional vocalizing is powerful for all types of imbalance; while looking in the mirror, individuals should speak slowly yet confidently, and repeat consciously selected, uplifting affirmations and mantras that engage the brain, and shift the subconscious mindset, such as the illumination at the start of this chapter. At the same time, they should pay direct focus to the vibrations of the vocal cords and chest, how the tongue touches the teeth and roof of the mouth while speaking, and how quickly the sound hits their ear drums. This will slow down, if not completely shut off, the mental noise of anxiety or fear, as the brain is given a subject to pay direct attention to. It strengthens awareness of the value of intentional language and the positive impact it makes, and serves as practice for expressing oneself through words in all of life's scenarios.

Because the throat chakra resonates with the color blue, people with underactive throat chakras will benefit by adding more blue to the color palette of their lives. They might add blue accents to their home decor, make blue butterfly pea flower tea, or add more blue clothing to their wardrobes. Adding more blue to the environment brings more peace to a space and awakens confidence. It soothes a body that is "stuck" with excessive amounts of stagnant energy buildup.

However, if the throat energy center is overactive, adding pops of the complementary color orange would be beneficial for adding warm energy to overabundant cool energy. Orange is energizing and as people with overactive throat chakras are often fatigued, it is clear why orange would be the color of choice for these individuals.

This color concept also applies to using crystals for improving energetic homoeostasis; adding a few orange crystals into the mix will provide the balance that some people with overactive throat chakras could benefit from. Remember, though, that how you choose to address an imbalance is dependent on how it shows up for someone, which can be very individualized.

As sound is linked to this energy center, it too can be used to bring balance into the throat chakra. Sound is a product of a vibrating object; energy is produced by the vibrations, which is then sent through a medium, such as air or water, in the form of sound waves. These sound waves stimulate vibrations in our ears that result in an electrical signal being produced and sent to the brain via the auditory nerve for interpretation. To simplify the matter, vibrations create more vibrations that impact their surroundings, including other people. Becoming conscious of the sound waves you absorb into your being is, therefore, an incredible way to get present quickly and find intentionality in the waves you create.

You may not always have the option to turn off the sounds you don't want to hear, such as car horns blaring in the distance, but you do have the choice to invite more peace into your life by focusing on what you want to listen to. For example, try nurturing moments of silence, adding your personal musical flair to the atmosphere or (and this is a very important one) stepping out of rooms filled with the language of negative, cynical people. By doing so, you will naturally begin to see the true value of sounds, thoughts and words, and the impact you can make with your own voice. Let it embolden you to share your own vocal sound waves, the carriers of your own vibration and frequency.

Vibration and frequency are two words that are often used in a spiritual sense, when describing how positive or negative something feels, but vibration and frequency also make up the world and how we experience it, as well as how we impact it. When you speak, the vibrations of your vocal cords send sound waves out to be received by those surrounding you. The quality and tone of these vibrations will inevitably determine how others will respond to you and, in this way, help to shape your own reality. We can harness this effect through the power of intention.

When intentionally using your voice and activating your hearing sense to create your reality, throat chakra crystals can assist in the process of merging mind and body through spirit, so you can more easily discover the truth of your expression. When working with your crystals, you can play with color by utilizing a variety of blue hues; maybe you want to use dark blue on days you seek to be more assertive and light blue for the intention of listening more intently to what others have to say. You might find yourself experimenting with partnering throat chakra and sacral chakra crystals, for example, to ignite a flame of directed energy in your articulation and make a stand-out impression on someone you meet for the first time.

Whatever your purpose, the overarching goal is to create a connection between your voice and the dynamic energy that throat chakra crystals carry. They hold your authentic expression in their structures, balancing it and sending it back to you in its most elevated

Sodalite

Lapis lazuli

form. Through this communication, you can come to understand the vibration and frequency of your own voice, and learn to take note of the vibrations and frequencies you bring home with you daily.

Crystals make for the perfect audience to share your thoughts and visions with. You can have practice conversations with them, recite speeches, prepare yourself with the confidence to ask for a raise, and even perfect your elevator pitch for that new business you want to create. There is no limit or judgment, but rather an open pathway for energy to be released and transmuted into the manifestation of your greatest destiny. As you continue to reach for your crystals, your clarity will heighten as you attune to the specific voice you programmed into your practice with them; it will continue to get better and better as time goes on.

Now that you are well-versed in the nature of the throat chakra and the role this energy center plays in your life, including how you communicate, your freedom to express yourself, your ability to connect with others, and even your creativity, it's time to take a moment for yourself. Gather your throat crystals and turn on the guided sound meditation audio. Observe the magnificent facets of your hearing, which provide you with the opportunity to experience a miracle of existence: the capability of processing, and becoming present with, the vibrations and frequencies that inform you of your surroundings, as well as what you contribute to them. This is the start of a journey into creating an environment of consistent growth, magic and aligned community through the intentional use of your voice and language. Get ready for a beautiful ride, my love.

Teal fluorite

THE FIFTH CRESCENDO

I would like to share with you one of my favorite exercises. This exercise is especially helpful for warming up your vocal cords prior to a speaking engagement, or when you want to achieve comfort with using your voice in an empowered way, no matter where you are and with whom you are speaking with.

1. Turn off electrical devices and lie down where you will not be disturbed for a few moments.

2. Now place a small and light throat chakra crystal in the hollow created by your collar bones. While gently tapping the crystal with your fingernail, begin to hum.

3. Start with a soft tone and quiet volume, and progressively increase the volume until you feel the vibrations of your voice from head to toe.

4. After you've moved through the spectrum of volume, tone and sound, choose where you felt most comfortable and alive, and continue humming in that sweet spot.

5. After about five minutes of humming like this, take a few long and deep breaths to relax any built-up tension that has migrated out toward the surface of your body.

6. Repeat the exercise until you are fully present and energy is flowing through your throat.

THROAT CHAKRA MEDITATION

Grab a soft pillow and get ready to press play on the sound healing track. Begin to hum and warm up your voice for a special exercise. While you do so, select the throat chakra crystals that resonate most with your vocal frequencies. Hold them in your hands. Prepare to begin.

Welcome to your throat chakra meditation. Lie on your back with your head on a soft pillow. The challenge is to stay fully awake, even in your comfort, while processing the sounds of the singing bowls, analyzing the way my voice comes into contact with your ear, and how the intonation in my words impact your emotions.

Now, hold one throat chakra crystal in each hand and place a small one near your throat, in between your collar bones. The only other thing you will be asked to do is repeat words after me, in the same volume and frequency, and explore how the different phrases and tones make you feel.

Have you tuned in to your breath today? The way the air sounds when it crosses into your nose and begins to fill your diaphragm and your lungs? Note the moment the air flows through your throat, bringing a cooling sensation to this energy center. In here lie the mechanisms of your voice – your most powerful tool for speaking language that creates your reality.

Picture yourself surrounded by a field of wild grasses and a blue sky. You are in communion with the nature around you; it is holding you, witnessing you and feeling your energy.

Take a long deep breath, in through your nose, and on your exhale, let out a deep sigh – one that is just loud enough to vibrate your throat and chest. Notice how those vibrations make you feel. Relaxed and relieved.

The wild grasses are graced with a sense of peace as your breath floats by and brushes against them. Imagine them gently swaying in the breeze of your air.

Try again now — except this time, breathe in through your nose and exhale from your mouth with a loud sigh. One that is primal and on the edge of screaming. Close your hands into a fist around your crystals. Think about a time you were too afraid to speak up for yourself, in childhood or adulthood.

Take another long deep breath, in through your nose, and exhale with an angry sigh.

That felt different, didn't it? Similar to a full body release, but also evoking memories where you may have felt stressed or upset. The wildlife pauses in fear and curiosity. The sky dims to a hue of grey.

You witnessed the impact of intention and directed energy.

Now, repeat the shadow statement after me:

I am unable to manifest the energy of my mind and thoughts into reality, using the sound waves of my voice. My words do not matter, or make an impact, so I keep my truth inside.

Repeat after me again, this time expressing the illumination statement:

I speak confidently and clearly, with dedication to my truth and authenticity. By doing so, I honor and uplift those for whom my message is an asset.

Which person do you want to be? Which statement creates the reality you want to achieve?

With both hands, touch the crystal between your collar bones gently.

Repeat "OM" three times with me — a sacred sound believed to connect with the Source energy of God. Start quietly and build in volume gradually — not with anger, but with truth, light and confidence. Pay attention to the vibrations reaching your fingertips through the crystal:

OM, OM, OM . . .

You are now the creator of your brightest destiny.

THIRD EYE CHAKRA

Key Themes:
Intuition, vision and perception

Element:
Light

Color:
Indigo

Color Psychology:
Mystery, intrigue, imagination, understanding, spirituality, relaxation

Sense: Intuition

No physical sense is associated with the Third Eye Chakra, as this is where we begin to journey beyond the boundaries of our physical form, and connect with the realms of existence that are not visible to the naked eye. These realms can be understood without the need for external validation, because they can be fully felt within the mind, body and spirit.

Body Awareness:
Pituitary gland, left eye, lower brain, nose, nervous system, ears, spine

Subtle Body Auric Layer:
Celestial body

SEVEN THIRD EYE CHAKRA CRYSTALS

Work with the following crystals to embody the illumination, open your third eye and perceive the layers of truth that lie beyond the physical realms.

1. Amethyst
2. Himalayan quartz
3. Purple labradorite
4. Azurite
5. Purple smithsonite
6. Lepidolite
7. Purple fluorite

AMETHYST
Spiritual awareness

Amethyst invites us to deepen our spiritual practices, quieting the mind, opening the heart and awakening the soul to the Divine Truth within us. Through this, we enhance our inner awareness, making it easier for us to use our intuition to navigate life with greater purpose and meaning, in alignment with our true self.

AZURITE
Intuition

Azurite enhances intuition and opens the third eye to facilitate the expansion of consciousness, thereby igniting the flame of curiosity that leads to self-discovery. Through this process, we become capable of discovering our inner truth, and utilizing it to make decisions that align with our highest good, follow our soul's calling and step into our fullest potential.

HIMALAYAN QUARTZ
Expansion

Himalayan quartz serves as a bridge to enlightenment by bringing alignment into our daily actions and expanding our ability to see beyond what appears immediately before our eyes. Himalayan quartz helps us to identify our strengths in the realm of consciousness and understanding, and illuminates the direct path to our highest potential by shining a light on how we can do better and be better, every day.

LEPIDOLITE
Trust

Lepidolite is similar to that of a tender embrace from an old friend who knows you better than anyone else. By tapping into this vast archive of wisdom and experience, we gain deeper insights into our purpose and the world around us. Lepidolite fosters self-trust, intuition and the ability to access ancient wisdom within us, enabling us to move confidently without fear or anxiety about the unknown.

PURPLE FLUORITE
Mental clarity

Purple fluorite, as a stone of focus and clarity, organizes scattered thoughts and improves concentration, helping to unlock our full cognitive abilities. It enables us to see the truth in all that is around us, and merges the information of the intuition with the clarity and logic of the mind, thereby reducing indecision and confusion. In other words, purple fluorite unites the intuition with the intellect, making us more intentional in our actions, and attracting success and fulfillment in all areas of life.

PURPLE LABRADORITE
Transformation

Purple labradorite is the crystal embodiment of "out with the old and in with the new." It accelerates the forward movement of change, leading to rapid personal development and spiritual expansion. Fear can often block the path to transformation, but purple labradorite breaks down such barriers and pushes us out of our comfort zones, inspiring us to welcome change with open arms. It encourages us to jump into the unknown, trusting that our path is unfolding exactly as it should and allowing us to step into new versions of our self with clear confidence.

PURPLE SMITHSONITE
Psychic insight

Purple smithsonite enhances our ability to open the doorway to Divine, spiritual knowledge that gives us insight into the subconscious, and discover that which may be holding us back from achieving our full potential. With its guidance, we can unlock the secrets to our true purpose and carve the path toward enlightenment. Purple smithsonite assists us to cut through illusions and see things for what they really are, empowering us to break free from our limitations and tap into our inner knowing.

THIRD EYE CRYSTAL SUBSTITUTES
Charoite, dumortierite, mystic merlinite, pietersite, sodalite, sugilite, tanzanite

CREATING BALANCE

You have set your intentions for balancing your third eye chakra and chosen which crystals you wish to work with. Now take note of the signs that will show whether you have achieved balance in your sixth energy center, or whether it remains imbalanced.

MANIFESTATIONS OF BALANCE

Mental	Healthy imagination | Intuitive decision-making | Creative thinking | Sound judgment | Open to diverse perspectives
Physical	High cognitive ability | Healthy eyesight | Instincts | Deep sleep | Good hormonal function
Emotional	Inspiration | Curiosity | Gratitude | Calm | Connection
Spiritual	Trust in oneself and one's life journey | Easily manifests intentions

MANIFESTATIONS OF IMBALANCE

Mental	Resistance to change | Lack of wisdom | Lack of clarity and focus | Inability to problem-solve | Disconnected from intuition
Physical	Headaches | Insomnia or nightmares | Vision problems and/or eye strain | Congestion and/or sinus infection | Allergies
Emotional	Confusion | Excessive fear | Overactive imagination | Paranoia | Lack of trust
Spiritual	Clogged perceptivity | Lack of intuitive understanding

THE THIRD EYE CHAKRA SEES THE WAY

Have you ever sensed a mysterious force guiding you toward a certain path in life? That's your intuition at work — an innate gift that is hardwired into all living beings. It's what helps us navigate the world, overcome challenges and find our sense of direction. It's a real and powerful sensation that can connect us to our spiritual nature and show us the way, even when the world around us is clouded in confusion and chaos. When we're born, we have a deep sense of who we are and what our purpose in life is. But as we grow up, society bombards us with endless options and opinions that can make us forget our true path. And that's where the third eye comes in — it helps us cut through the noise and reconnect with our spiritual core.

Connecting with the third eye can feel like a challenging task, so knowing where it is located within your body can be incredibly helpful. If you place your finger on your forehead, right in between your eyebrows, you are touching the spot where your sixth energy center resides. This powerful chakra is responsible for governing various aspects of your spiritual being, including your intuition, insight, imagination and wisdom. It is also associated with the color indigo, a stunning blend of royal blue and purple that is known for its incredible spiritual properties.

Many people automatically assume that the third eye is connected to the pineal gland, which is often

Amethyst

referred to as the "seat of the soul." However, it is most closely connected to the pituitary gland. This tiny gland is also known as the "master gland" and it releases a variety of important hormones such as growth hormone, prolactin, thyroid-stimulating hormone and more. It also works in tandem with the hypothalamus to regulate the body's internal environment and controls the overall endocrine system that governs the thyroid, ovaries/testes and adrenals. These glands are all linked to the lower chakras, making the pituitary gland and third eye chakra the epicenter where our physical and spiritual selves merge.

The third eye chakra's impact on our perspective and perception is profound. It allows us to go beyond the surface and see the bigger picture, becoming aware of our true selves and our place in the Universe. Similarly, the pituitary gland plays a vital role in our growth and development throughout our lives, ensuring that we fulfill our potential as human beings on this earth. When our third eye chakra is balanced and healthy, it works just like the pituitary gland, guiding us toward spiritual growth and transformation, and helping us fulfill our destiny.

But that's not all – the third eye also governs the lower brain, nose, left eye, ears and nervous system. The nervous system handles almost everything we do and feel, including our thoughts and memory, which are directly linked to the health

Purple fluorite

of our third eye chakra. While our nervous system serves as our physical gauge, constantly monitoring bodily functions and keeping everything running smoothly, the third eye is your spiritual gauge — it works in tandem with your nervous system to create a complete picture of your overall wellbeing. Nestled between our two physical eyes, the third eye chakra serves as the gateway to the spiritual realm, allowing us to perceive and connect with the world beyond the physical.

While our two physical eyes take in our surroundings, it is through the third eye that we gain insight into our deeper self and connect with others on a soul level. When we lock eyes with someone, we often feel as though we're peering into their soul, but we rarely acknowledge the connection that our third eyes are forging in that moment. This is where our intuition kicks in, helping us determine whether the person we're connecting with is trustworthy or someone we're meant to build a deeper bond with. Perhaps you've experienced that inexplicable feeling of familiarity when meeting someone new, as though you've crossed paths before? This is the work of a healthy third eye, tapping into the vibrational frequency that already entangles your energy with another. Making eye contact may seem daunting at first, but with practice and with the right people, it becomes easier to experience the power of true connection. Making eye contact is not only a signal to your third eye to activate, but also a signal to your brain that you are confident and intentional with every move you make, which then encourages you to live a more aligned and intentional daily life.

As spiritual beings having a human experience, it's important for us to embrace the physical aspects of life. But without the clarity provided by the third eye, we risk losing sight of our ultimate mission on this earth. We may find ourselves wandering down a path with no clear direction, feeling lost and disconnected. By trusting our intuition and tapping into the wisdom of the third eye, we stay connected to our inner knowing and spiritual nature.

One of the most amazing aspects of a balanced third eye chakra is the gift of imagination. With a clear and open third eye, there are no limits to what the mind can visualize, create and experience. Thanks to their almost otherworldly manifestation skills, third eye warriors are able to manifest their visions with ease. They don't hesitate about what they want or whether they deserve it — they simply bring it into the present because they already have it in another timeline. But the benefits of a balanced third eye chakra go far beyond manifestation skills. These individuals are capable of achieving deep spiritual states that teach and grow them in ways that are truly profound. They are able to connect with the Universe on a level that most people can only dream of, and they use this connection to create positive change in their lives, as well as the lives of those around them. When your own sixth energy center is vibrating at its optimal frequency, you will experience a level of clarity that transcends the mundane and ordinary.

KNOWING YOUR PURPOSE

Individuals with a balanced third eye chakra know who they are and move through life with a sense of direction that is inspiring. They radiate an energy that is undeniable and motivating, making the impossible seem achievable with ease.

Their journey serves as a guiding light for those who may have thought that such success was beyond their reach. These individuals are therefore often found in roles where they can serve as spiritual guides or teachers, driven by a passion for helping others achieve self-awareness and spiritual growth. Their intuition is finely tuned, and they are drawn toward mystical studies such as astrology, as well as creative pursuits that allow them to express themselves.

They are natural problem-solvers, using their vivid imaginations to find solutions that others may not have even considered. Their creativity is unmatched, and they can bring ideas to life in unique ways that lead others to wonder "how in the world did they come up with that?" That is because they are not of this world. The beauty of these individuals is that they can excel at any role they choose, driven by their deep sense of purpose and an unwavering commitment to living a fulfilling life. Being around them is truly an experience, and it's no wonder that they leave a lasting impact on everyone they encounter.

Relationships with individuals who have balanced third eye chakras are truly remarkable and unforgettable. They have an uncanny ability to serve as a reflection for their loved ones, providing them with a broader perspective and helping them to see the endless possibilities for their lives. These individuals possess a deep

Azurite

Lepidolite

Purple smithsonite

Purple labradorite

understanding of the human experience, yet they also possess the unique ability to see beyond the physical realm, recognizing the infinite potential of each person as a spiritual being capable of transformation and evolution. As creative beings, people with balanced third eye chakras tend to have vibrant and exciting relationships that are driven by a mutual thirst for adventure and a desire to explore the many facets of love, connection and the Universe. They inspire their loved ones to embrace their inner adventurer and live life to the fullest, while simultaneously raising their vibrational frequencies to new heights, propelling them toward their highest selves and purpose-driven lives.

Although they value and cherish relationships, these individuals are also fiercely independent and self-sufficient, empowering their partners and loved ones to be their authentic selves in the world. All in all, being in a relationship with someone with a balanced third eye chakra is truly a transformative experience that will leave a lasting impact on your life by guiding you, and inspiring you, toward your own vibrantly illuminated path.

LIGHTING THE WAY

When the third eye chakra is out of balance, the impact on an individual's spiritual and physical wellbeing can be drastic. It is like walking around with a cloud hanging over your head, making it challenging to process thoughts and form coherent ideas. Those suffering from an imbalanced third eye chakra often experience consistent headaches, sometimes leading to serious and insufferable migraines. Their lack of focus and direction can leave them feeling lost and confused, suffering from brain fog and indecisiveness. Their intuition is stifled, leaving them unable to tap into their inner guidance when they need it most. They can't be there for others as a source of motivation and inspiration, and often feel completely disconnected from life. This sense of disconnection can lead to unbearable anxiety and depression, making it difficult to find meaning and purpose in life. The loneliness can be suffocating, and the lack of self-understanding and purpose can be deeply unsettling. In short, an imbalanced third eye chakra can have a profound impact on every aspect of an individual's life. It can leave them feeling lost, alone and disconnected from the world around them.

Imbalances can occur in childhood when children are taught to suppress their intuition and inner voice. Instead of nurturing this gift and allowing it to flourish, authoritarian parents often rob their children of this essential skill. Moreover, excessive early exposure to heavily scripted media and programming can also have a negative impact on the third eye chakra. These manipulative influences can program our subconscious, overriding the innate capabilities of our third eye to perceive and process our own thoughts and understanding. This leads to a loss of autonomy and individual thought, where other people or corporations dictate what we should be and do. In both cases, the third eye chakra falls out of alignment, leading to negative impacts on our mind, body and spirit. It's crucial to protect and nurture our sixth energy center by encouraging individual thought, curiosity and intuition. By doing so, we can stay true to our authentic selves and achieve optimal energetic balance.

I have come across numerous situations where clients have developed dysregulated nervous systems. Although the source of dysregulation may not be apparent, its effects can be felt strongly as the senses are often overstimulated even in everyday situations, making everything feel overwhelming. Their minds are racing a mile a minute, making it hard to stay present in reality. As a coping mechanism, many people tend to daydream excessively to cushion their brains from further stimulation. While this might offer temporary relief, it overloads the third eye chakra, resulting in too much influx, with not enough room for action or processing. Insomnia is another common issue for those with an overactive third eye chakra, where clients struggle to fall asleep or stay asleep, perpetuating the cycle of overstimulation and exhaustion.

An excellent technique for managing an overactive third eye chakra is to focus on your breath. By slowing down your breathing and bringing your awareness deeper into your body, you can quiet the constant chatter of your mind and become more grounded. A great way to do this is by attending breathwork classes, where you can participate in rhythmic breathing exercises, meditation and even movement to help you shift through emotional blockages.

But you don't have to attend a class to practice breathwork. One of my favorite exercises is the 4-7-8 breath. This simple technique involves inhaling through your nose for four seconds, holding your breath for seven seconds and then exhaling through your mouth for eight seconds. Not only does this exercise help to calm the body and reduce stress and anxiety, but it improves focus and mental clarity. Next time you are overwhelmed and the weight of the world feels like it is crashing down on you, and you're not sure you will make it through another day, take a few deep breaths. Try the 4-7-8 breath exercise to bring yourself back into balance and remember who you really are.

When it comes to an underactive third eye chakra, where energy isn't flowing freely, I have noticed that one of the most common culprits is poor nutrition in childhood that lingers into adulthood. These people continue to consume diets that are detrimental to their wellbeing and energy levels, making it difficult to connect with their spiritual inner knowing and vision. Instead, their bodies and minds become fixated on removing toxicity from the body, making their energy dense and heavy. It's no secret that food has a significant impact on the body, and when it doesn't receive the proper input, the endocrine system suffers, causing systems to go out of balance and health issues to arise. This holds especially true for the pituitary gland, the "master gland" that governs many hormone-secreting glands. When it's treated with disregard, the damage can take years to reverse, and the communication and interconnectedness of mind, body and spirit all suffer. While it's essential to recognize the link between food quality and

Himalayan quartz

chakra balance for all energy centers, this is particularly true for the third eye chakra, as it's responsible for our perception of reality and our spiritual growth.

Besides adjusting your diet, an effective approach to healing and balancing this chakra is to bring light into your life in new and creative ways, even if you just throw open your curtains and bask in the warmth of the Sun's rays. Not only will this help boost your mood, but it will also allow your third eye to soak up all that lovely golden energy. But why stop at natural light when you can experiment with a powerful combination of color and light? If you want to target your third eye specifically, try incorporating indigo-colored LED lights and crystals into your space. This can help activate and strengthen this energy center, allowing you to tap into your intuition and inner wisdom like never before. However, if you're dealing with an overactive third eye and need to slow things down a bit, consider creating some darkness in your space. This can be especially helpful at night when you're trying to wind down and get some rest. Instead of harsh blue or white lights, mix in soothing yellow and orange tones. These colors are actually the opposite of indigo on the color wheel and can help balance out any excessive energy in your third eye.

As the first of the two chakras that aren't linked to a physical sense, the sixth energy center holds a unique and powerful position in our spiritual bodies. It's not something we can touch or see, but rather an innate part of who we are. Activating the third eye sense of intuition isn't about learning something new, but about remembering something old — coming back home to ourselves and rediscovering our true essence. By strengthening and enhancing what's already within us, we can awaken the magic of our intuition like never before. The inner vision, cycled through the portal of the third eye, *is* the intuition and it is through this energy center that we finally begin to see truly, once again. It's time to tap into the infinite wisdom that resides within us all, and the Gem Sorcery Method intends to help you get there.

Before we begin the visualization and meditation that follow, take a moment to prepare your sacred space and create an environment that fosters stillness and inner peace. Allow yourself ample time to immerse yourself fully in this experience and connect with your Higher Self. Bring your favorite third eye crystals with you, as companions for the journey. As we embark on this path of self-discovery, may you be filled with spiritual light and profound revelations . . .

WRITE YOURSELF AN ADVENTURE

This exercise is designed to activate an underactive third eye chakra. It is meant to stimulate your creativity, provide clarity in your purpose, and energize your third eye chakra by letting your Inner Child take the reins.

1. Select a crystal that corresponds to the third eye chakra and find a comfortable position to lie on the ground. Place the crystal on your forehead, between your eyebrows, and over your third eye energy center.

2. Now, it's time to let your imagination run wild! Picture yourself as a character in a fairy tale or fiction story, and envision an exciting and imaginative environment around you. Let your creativity flow and make the environment as wild and vibrant as possible. Tap into your inner childlike joy and creativity.

3. Next, it's time to tell your story. Describe yourself, your surroundings and your storyline in detail, as if you were writing a novel. Record your voice with your phone or other device to capture your story. If you wish, you can write it down afterwards in your Gem Sorcery journal.

4. Each time you do this exercise, pick up where you left off and continue building on your story. Over time, you'll find that you've created an entire novel that uncovers your true purpose through your imagination.

THIRD EYE CHAKRA MEDITATION

If you haven't already, play around with the lighting in your space, choosing the color or brightness that deepens your inner connection. Trust your intuition to pick the crystal(s) for this journey. Your spirit knows the right one. Keep a pillow handy for head support as you journey through your generational history. Prepare to begin.

Welcome to your third eye meditation. Place a cushion or pillow beneath your head and bend your legs, so that the bottoms of your feet are touching. Gently set a small third eye crystal between your eyebrows and upon your third eye. Place your hands on the ground beside you with your palms facing up toward the sky.

Before you begin to tune in to your intuition and channel the wisdom of the Divine, pay close attention to the edges of your physical form and consciousness. Feel your body's density, sinking heavily into the ground or earth below you. You are going to stay anchored to this physical form, as you begin to float gently into a state of conscious intuition and channel the wisdom of the Universe.

But first, sit in the heaviness of the physical for a few breaths. Close your eyes. Breathe in through your nose, and exhale out of your mouth . . . becoming heavier and heavier with every breath. Two more times, inhale . . . exhale. One more time, inhale . . . exhale. You should feel as heavy as a paperweight at this point.

Now, begin to distinguish the lightness of your spirit from the density of your body. Your spirit is a fluttery and airy energy that lingers at the boundaries of the physical. It extends outward from your body, coming into contact with all vibrational frequencies and energies that surround you.

Picture this force field, your aura, growing bigger and brighter until it fills the room in its entirety. Now, notice how you are beginning to float as free as a feather, your spirit gently drifting away from your body.

*Draw the light from your aura back inward, toward the very center
of your forehead until it is concentrated in the crystal there.*

*The energy at your third eye begins to build up intensely until
it channels itself into a focused beam of indigo-colored light,
reaching the heavens and extending out to connect to all forms
of ancient wisdom, and imprint these onto your intuition.*

*Strands of your DNA appear before you, lit up brightly and carrying the
information of multiple generations past. They slowly begin to unravel,
and as they do so, the stories of your infinite existence are revealed.*

*Fully connected, you begin to see the truth – your truth – and all
lifetimes you've lived that developed your current awareness and
incarnation. They play before you like a home movie – every conception,
every birth earth-side, every relationship, and every passing.*

Everything you need is within you NOW. Claim it and . . . repeat after me:

With a clear and focused mind, I perceive the world around
me with heightened intuition and deep understanding,
trusting my inner wisdom to guide me on my path.

*Your indigo third eye beam gently descends from the realm
of the Divine to reincorporate with the crystal . . .*

*And slowly disperses as light across the edges and boundaries of
your physical existence, where body and spirit connect. You become
dense again, ready to merge back into the earthly realm.*

*Everything you need is within you NOW. Move in the grace,
gratitude and awareness of your truth, for it is your guiding light.*

SHADOW

*"Disconnected from the spiritual realm,
I feel lost and aimless, struggling to find
meaning and purpose in my life."*

ILLUMINATION

*"Connected to the Divine and the infinite Universe,
I am filled with boundless spiritual energy, experiencing
inner peace and a sense of oneness with all that exists."*

CROWN CHAKRA

Key Themes:
Divinity, unity and wisdom

Element:
Pure awareness

Color:
Violet or white

Color Psychology:
Divinity, luxury, royalty, mysticism, originality, possibility

Sense: Universal consciousness

Like the third eye chakra, no physical sense is associated with the crown chakra. It is connected to pure, unfiltered awareness. This awareness ties us to the Universal Consciousness, which flows through all things. It is the same energy that makes up everything around us, from the trees in the garden to the air we breathe. Just like the flowers in the garden that bloom and eventually wilt, our physical bodies will also return to the earth. But the energy that we consist of will be dispersed back into the Universe, becoming a part of the vast cosmic energy that surrounds us all.

Body Awareness:
Upper skull and brain, right eye, cerebral cortex, pineal gland, nervous system, endocrine system

Subtle Body Auric Layer:
Causal body

SEVEN CROWN CHAKRA CRYSTALS

These seven crystals bring purity and wonder, embodying the illumination and lighting the way to connection with the Universal Consciousness.

1. Selenite
2. Clear fluorite
3. Scolecite
4. Clear quartz
5. Spirit quartz
6. Garden quartz
7. White calcite

CLEAR FLUORITE
Surrender

Clear fluorite provides the inspiration to release control and surrender to the natural cycles of life. It encourages us to be fully present within the now. Clear fluorite helps us to release our attachment to outcomes and, instead, live in the beauty of ever-flowing creation and transformation. This state of surrender brings a sense of freedom and allows us to experience the joy of simply being alive.

CLEAR QUARTZ
Amplification

Clear quartz not only clears but amplifies the energy of the body. By purifying negative energy and transforming it into positivity, clear quartz paves the way for powerful manifestation and the realization of our greatest intentions. It magnifies our strengths and illuminates our potential, reminding us of our innate connection to the magic of the Universe.

GARDEN QUARTZ
Magic

Garden quartz imbues life with awe, enchantment and wonder, inspiring us to see the magic that surrounds us every day. By opening our consciousness to the mystical aspects of the Universe, it helps us to recognize the serendipitous moments that align with our soul's path. Garden quartz reminds us that we are capable of creating magic and invites us to live a life filled with a deep sense of possibility.

SCOLECITE
Unity

Scolecite establishes deeper and stronger connections with those around us, fostering an environment of empathy, compassion and understanding. Its high vibrational energy creates a space for harmony, helping us to break down the barriers of separation. It opens us up to the beauty of unity, while showing us how to work together for positive change to make the world a better place for all.

SELENITE
Tranquility

Selenite has a purifying energy that clears the mind of the negative energy that traps us in the depths of isolation. As its radiance illuminates the darkness within us, we are able to transform negative thought patterns into positive energy, leading to a calming connection with the Divine. Selenite's bright reflection of light invites us to embrace a new perspective and find tranquility in the present moment.

SPIRIT QUARTZ
Mystery

Spirit quartz guides us to surrender to the enigmatic nature of existence and have faith in God's grand design, whatever God looks like for us. It inspires us to find wonder in the intricacies of life, appreciating every detail, regardless of how it fits into our personal plans. Every moment is a precious gift, and spirit quartz encourages us to cherish each one, even when we cannot comprehend its significance in the grand scheme of things.

WHITE CALCITE
Spiritual purity

White calcite is like a beam of pure, high vibrational energy that clears the energetic pathway connecting us to the Divine Universal Consciousness. It sheds light on the human ego, so that it may be transformed into something more beautiful and allow us to surrender to the natural flow of life. Through this perspective, we see that we are truly connected and there is no need for judgment or separation. White calcite helps us to recognize that we all share the same needs and desires, and that we are all expressions of the limitless potential of the Universe.

CROWN CRYSTAL SUBSTITUTES

Apophyllite, clear topaz, danburite, howlite, labradorite, phenacite, rainbow moonstone

CREATING BALANCE

When you have chosen your crystal(s) and set your intention to balance your crown chakra, be aware of the following indicators, which will show whether you have achieved balance in your seventh energy center, or whether it remains imbalanced.

MANIFESTATIONS OF BALANCE

Mental	Deep understanding of self | Realization of the spiritual | Intuition | Belonging and oneness | Potent expression
Physical	Enhanced memory | Deep sleep | New neurological connections | Reduced stress | Lack of headaches
Emotional	Peace | Humility | Serenity | Bliss | Gratitude
Spiritual	Awareness of synchronicities | Expanded sense of gratitude for the Now

MANIFESTATIONS OF IMBALANCE

Mental	Self-importance | Unproductive rumination | Inability to think critically | Spirituality as a means of avoidance | Dissociation from thoughts
Physical	Dizziness | Sensitivity to environment | Overactive thoughts | Depression | Physical and mental tension
Emotional	Loneliness | Fear | Discontentment | Obsession | Distress
Spiritual	Grandiose sense of spiritual superiority | Feelings of isolation

THE CROWN CHAKRA CONNECTS WITH THE DIVINE

Imagine a world where everything is interconnected, and each individual is a part of a greater whole. This is the essence of the Universal Consciousness, also known as the Cosmic Consciousness, or the Divine Consciousness. It implies that there is a higher purpose to our existence and that we can gain profound insights into the nature of reality by accessing this plane of being. As we delve deeper into understanding our connection with the Universal Consciousness, we learn to see the crown chakra as an antenna that receives messages from the Divine. These messages help us to better understand our human form and the purpose of our existence.

However, in order to access this Divine knowledge, we must balance and activate the first six chakras, clearing any blockages along the way, before we reach the seventh energy center. The closer we get to the crown chakra, the closer we are to achieving full alignment with our divinity. It is in this space where duality fades away, and everything simply is . . . and isn't. It's where our oneness with all creation becomes apparent.

White calcite

The crown chakra, located at the very top of the head, is like a gateway to the transcendental — a level of existence that exceeds the limits of our everyday human experience. It's the place where we can embody enlightenment and connect with something greater than ourselves. This energy center is often represented by the color violet or white, and is closely associated with the pineal gland, also known as the "seat of the soul." This tiny gland, located in the center of the brain, is responsible for regulating our sleep–wake cycle by producing melatonin. And when we sleep, we lose our perception of the physical body and become one with everything around us. We're not weighed down by stress or responsibilities, and we're free to dream and explore altered states of consciousness. It's truly a gift from the pineal gland, which is why it's no surprise that this part of the body is associated with the crown chakra.

It has also been discovered that low levels of melatonin are linked to depression, a feeling that can leave us feeling helpless and disconnected from the world around us. In those dark moments, it can be hard to see beyond the immediate feelings of loneliness and despair, let alone recognize our place in something greater than ourselves. But if we can muster the strength to take just one small step toward balancing our crown chakra, the benefits that arise in both our physical and spiritual bodies can lead us toward a more fulfilling life and a sense of connectedness to the world.

The pineal gland also plays a crucial role in our reproductive and immune systems, thanks in part to the anti-inflammatory and antioxidant effects of melatonin. This energy center also governs the cerebral cortex, the right eye and the endocrine and nervous systems. It's like the conductor of a symphony, orchestrating the flow of energy throughout the body and allowing us to tap into our spiritual nature.

The crown chakra is the portal to an awe-inspiring sense of purpose and fulfillment that extends beyond ourselves. When this chakra is balanced, we feel connected to this greater purpose and experience a profound sense of wholeness, as if we lack nothing. Imagine living in a constant state of bliss, feeling grateful for what we have and understanding our place in the world — that's the power of a balanced crown chakra.

As humans, we have a natural inclination to look down when we feel bogged down by life's burdens. When we're weighed down by heavy emotions and the never-ending stresses of daily living, it's all too easy to focus on the ground beneath our feet and the endless chasm that separates us from others. But what if we looked up instead? What if we stood tall, with our heads held high, and opened ourselves up to the boundless possibilities that await us in the heavens? This is where the crown chakra comes in: located at the very top of our heads, it invites us to stand tall and look toward the sky. It encourages us to open ourselves up to the messages of the Divine, to trust in

Garden quartz

Clear fluorite

the Universe, and to welcome synchronicity and understanding into our lives. It takes courage to look up and trust in something beyond ourselves, but when we do, the rewards are immeasurable. We become connected to something greater than ourselves, and we're able to see the world in a new light. Our stresses melt away and we are met with the miracle of simply being alive.

EMBODYING CALM AND CONNECTION

People with balanced crown chakras have a deep understanding of themselves and the world around them, and maintain a sense of tranquility and calm. They exude a natural energy of wisdom and grace. These individuals have a special aura about them — one that exudes awareness and experience that seems to span beyond just one lifetime. When you're lucky enough to meet them, they stand out in a crowd, like a shining beacon in the darkness. They have an innate ability to see things differently and find solutions to even the most complex problems. It is as though they have a sixth sense that allows them to tap into the deeper meaning of life and see through the distractions that plague the rest of us. They are not bogged down by analysis or indecision. Instead, they know how to move forward with purpose and strength, always finding a way through even the most challenging situations.

These people have a natural inclination to become spiritual teachers and mentors, sharing their wisdom with others in order to help them achieve a state of enlightenment and connectedness, too. You'll often find them practicing reiki healing and other therapeutic techniques, as they're passionate about understanding the energetic nature of the human body and the power of healing through the integration of mind, body and spirit. But their impact goes far beyond just one-on-one interactions. These individuals often become leaders in their communities, inspiring others to embrace a more meaningful existence and showing them the path to a greater sense of purpose. And when you're around them, you can't help but feel that there's something more to life than just the day-to-day grind.

Once in a blue moon, you may find yourself fortunate enough to be in a relationship with someone whose crown chakra is perfectly balanced. These individuals radiate gratitude and are deeply committed to their connection with the Divine Consciousness. Being around them is like being enveloped in a warm blanket of compassion and empathy. They do not pass judgment and find it impossible not to be grateful for the miracle of existence. In a relationship with them, you will be showered with an abundance of love and respect. As you share your passion for the beauty of life, your bond will deepen, and your connection will become stronger. They are considerate of your needs and desires because they view everything through the lens of the Universal Consciousness. For them, the phrase "we are all one" is not just a catchphrase, but a way of life. They don't take offense at anything because they understand that everything is as it should be. However, being in a relationship with someone who is so fully present can be uncomfortable, particularly if you are still carrying

Scolecite

your own triggers and traumas. But once you open up to this level of unconditional love, the relationship becomes unbreakable, lasting until the end of time. It truly is a blessing to find yourself in a relationship with one of these rare, beautiful souls.

On the other hand, many of us are likely to meet individuals with imbalanced crown chakras, which can lead to cynicism, a lack of faith and closed-mindedness. These people may find themselves unable to see any meaning in life, which can be incredibly isolating and lonely. In addition to cynicism, an imbalanced crown chakra can also result in analysis paralysis. This is where overthinking leads to a complete inability to make decisions or take major steps forward. Opportunities slip away, and these individuals become trapped in a cycle of inaction and negative thinking; however, with awareness, they can find a renewed sense of fulfillment in their lives.

Sometimes it's depression that throws us off balance and takes us down, making it hard to see the light at the end of the tunnel. But other scenarios can affect us too, without us realizing it until we're already feeling the weight of their imbalance on our seventh energy center. Picture this: you're someone who believes in the power of love and the importance of connection. But you've been made fun of for your beliefs. People call you a "hippie" or say you're out of touch with reality. And slowly but surely, you start to feel like maybe they are right. Maybe you are just a little too "woo-woo" for this world? Or maybe you're someone who's been overexposed to the media, whose divisive rhetoric starts to seep into your consciousness, making you feel unsafe in this world, and so you shut off the loving and open part of yourself. You start to see people as "others"

Selenite

rather than valuable pieces of the collective. And before you know it, you become harsh and cold, unable to bring open-mindedness to other perspectives.

Sometimes the seventh energy center can be adversely affected if we grew up in a divisive environment, where open-mindedness was not encouraged and other thought systems or beliefs were judged to be wrong. I see this often in my work with clients, especially those individuals who had parents who were emotionally unavailable and whose home life was far from stable. Growing up without a guide or mentor to nurture your growth and evolution can be a lonely and confusing experience, leaving you adrift in the world, struggling to find your place. If your parents fought a lot, this can cause you to feel anxious and withdraw, searching for safety and stability that never seem to come. In this state of withdrawal, you may lose sight of who you are and stop trusting that anyone is out there for you. Without a sense of purpose or direction, these individuals often find themselves getting into trouble, falling into depression and lacking motivation. Subconsciously, they model their parents' behavior, perpetuating the chaos and turmoil that their parents placed them in as young children.

This lack of self-awareness keeps the crown chakra underactive, making these people feel even more alone and lost. It's heartbreaking to see individuals who have had to navigate this kind of childhood. But by working on nurturing and balancing the crown chakra, it is possible to break free from the patterns of the past and rewrite their story.

When I encounter individuals who are struggling with an underactive crown chakra, they often have a missing link needed to connect with their Higher Selves and the Universe. To help them, I use a powerful visualization exercise that begins by asking them to envision a brilliant white beam of light descending from the heavens and meeting them at the top of their heads. As they continue to imagine the light, they will start to feel a cooling sensation that begins as a tingle on the surface of their skull and gradually spreads throughout their entire body. By taking deep breaths through the nose and exhaling through the mouth, they can help the white light to travel through each of their chakras — starting with the crown and continuing down to the root chakra — filling their body with that cooling, activating light from head to toe. The white light that they imagine is the Universal Consciousness, containing all of the messages and knowledge of the universe, and activating and balancing each and every chakra. This visualization exercise can help to connect individuals with their Higher Selves and the greater whole of the Universe. Additionally, if the client feels drawn to it, I encourage them to place a crown chakra crystal such as clear quartz at the top of their head to amplify the energy of this practice.

Similar to the third eye chakra, the crown chakra can be balanced anywhere, anytime, whether you're surrounded by people or on your own. The ultimate goal is to achieve balance and make it a natural state of your being. However, there are tools that can help you along the way. Crystals and color therapy, for instance, can be extremely useful in balancing your seventh chakra, whether it is overactive or, indeed, underactive.

PERFECT BALANCE

Have you ever met someone who seems to think that they are spiritually above everyone else? They carry themselves with an air of superiority, believing that their path is the only correct path and that everyone else is misguided. These individuals often have a backstory of finding spirituality at a time when they needed it most, and they were so inspired by the positive impact it had on their lives that they fell headfirst into it. At first, this newfound passion is a beautiful thing to witness, but then they become obsessed with their spiritual practices, to the point where they are out of touch with the realities of the physical world. As they become more detached and disassociated, their relationships, jobs and conversations become unenjoyable because they don't align with their spiritual practices. Their spirituality becomes their entire identity, and they become arrogant, refusing to acknowledge any other belief system as worthy. Their life starts to unravel. They're living in the physical world, and they have responsibilities that need to be addressed in order to achieve spiritual and physical balance. Neglecting their responsibilities leads to a destructive cycle that is difficult to escape.

This inflated sense of self and detachment from reality is a telltale sign of an overactive crown chakra and can be just as damaging as not having a spiritual guide, or being made to feel ashamed of one's beliefs. It's helpful to find a balance between our spiritual practices and the physical world we inhabit.

So, if your crown chakra is overactive, what can you do? Well, it's essential to utilize the color yellow to balance out the violet energy of the crown chakra. Yellow crystals like citrine and amber can be your go-to. At the other end of the spectrum, if your crown chakra is underactive, you might want to surround yourself with violet crystals, violet art and even wear violet clothes to activate this energy center. Also remember to ensure that all your other chakras have been balanced, as we approach the end of our journey in these pages . . .

Spirit quartz

Clear quartz

Congratulations on reaching the final stage of the seven primary chakras! It takes immense dedication and effort to make it this far, and I'm truly proud of you. The journey has not been easy, but the rewards that come with harmonizing all seven chakras are simply life-changing.

As we embark on this final leg of the experience, I invite you to behold the ultimate sensation of bliss and connectedness. We will work toward bringing every single one of your chakras into perfect harmony, creating a symphony of energy that flows seamlessly through your body. Once we're finished, I will show you how to integrate everything you've learned about Gem Sorcery into your daily life, so you can always access a state of balance no matter where you are. But for now, take a moment to gather your crown chakra crystals, find a quiet and comfortable space where you can fully release and become one with your world. The crown chakra may be the final stop, but it is also the beginning of a whole new world of possibilities. Let's explore this together and see what wonders we can discover.

TREE GROUNDING

This is a wonderful exercise that I use to help individuals with overactive crown chakras. These individuals are so caught up in their spiritual pursuits that they lose touch with the physical world. They may feel like they're floating away into the ethers, disconnected from the earth beneath their feet. For those of us who have been neglecting the physical elements of our being, this exercise can change everything.

1. To ground yourself, place your bare feet on the earth — on dirt or a wet forest floor, if possible.

2. Now take a few deep breaths and imagine roots extending from the bottom of your feet, burying themselves deep into the earth. These roots give you strength and stability. They prevent you from floating away and allow you to focus on what's right in front of you.

3. Release any excess mental energy into the earth, allowing all your worries and distractions to flow down into the soil.

4. In exchange, absorb the grounding energy of the earth back into your being. Take deep breaths, inhaling and exhaling, while you create a beneficial circulation of energy, releasing what no longer serves you and absorbing energy to ground yourself.

5. When you are ready, go about your day with steadfast commitment to the here and now

CROWN CHAKRA MEDITATION

To fully engage in this experience, seek a distraction-free space. You do not need to do much other than be fully present in your surroundings. Grab a soft cushion, allowing for utmost comfort and the freedom to detach from your physical form. Surround yourself with at least four crown chakra crystals: front, left, right and back. (If you have more than four crystals, surround yourself with a full circle.) Prepare to begin.

Welcome to your crown chakra meditation. Sit on your cushion with your legs crossed, or your knees bent with the bottoms of your feet touching one another. Place your hands on your knees with your index fingertips touching and your palms facing upwards toward the sky. Note the crystal energy surrounding you, vibrating and aligning each of your energy centers into a state of true harmony.

Do you remember when you first began this transformative and sacred journey? Rooting yourself into the earth, setting a strong foundation for the work you were about to do. Exploring and vibing with each of your physical senses, coming to know yourself more intimately than ever before, and opening in ways you never thought possible.

Close your eyes and meditate on this thought. It's amazing, isn't it? How truly connected we are to the Universe in its entirety?

Keeping your eyes closed, inhale deeply, becoming fully connected to your breath. As you continue to breathe, allow your breath to come from lower and lower in your body, until it originates at your perineum.

A gently spinning red light begins to emanate there, and with each new inhale, you activate the spinning wheel of the subsequent energy center, stacking them upon each other.

Orange light appears just below your naval . . . Then yellow, at your diaphragm. Green in your heart center . . . Blue at your throat . . . Indigo directly in the center of your eyebrows . . . And finally, pure white light right at the crown of your head.

With each wheel spinning, intense energy rises up from the root,
through the sacral, then solar plexus and heart; through the throat,
into the third eye, and OUT . . . from the top of your head.

Behind your eyelids is a psychedelic kaleidoscope of colors forming brilliant shapes and
patterns and then . . . everything goes white, filling your entire scope of perception with the
brightest light you've ever seen. The air chills and your body begins to shift into particle
matter, slowly dispersing to merge with the Collective Consciousness. Your memories, your
beliefs, your belongings imprint themselves on the Collective Consciousness with you.

Now, repeat after me:

Connected to the Divine and infinite Universe, I am filled with boundless spiritual
energy, experiencing inner peace and a sense of oneness with all that exists.

You are free, yet fully integrated with the spiritual awareness of the Collective Consciousness.

Stay here, or should I say here and nowhere, for 20 seconds.

Now, take a deep breath and prepare yourself to witness
the last several moments, moving in reverse.

Every particle of you that drifted out into the ether returns, and you
are placed back together like a complex puzzle piece, perfectly
aligned, quite possibly even more so than before.

As each particle integrates back into your physical form, the air
becomes warm and you tune in to your heart beating gently in
your chest and your blood flowing through your veins.

Bringing life to the physical body, full of arteries, bones, cartilage and flesh.

You. Are. Human.

You. Are. Spirit.

You. Are. A Miracle.

More whole than ever before, you are free.

CONCLUSION

The practices we embarked upon together in these pages are more than just exercises: they hold the power to awaken your senses, ignite your spirit and anchor you in the present moment. They are the keys that unlock the door to a new way of being. Like a symphony, these rituals are meant to be played and replayed, until they become a part of you. At first, it might feel foreign, like working out new muscles. That's because your brain undergoes a transformation in adopting the illumination mindsets as your truth. Intentional actions meant to change your brain become habits that shift your reality. You emerge from this metamorphosis as someone entirely new, intimately connected to your body and profoundly aware of the intricate dance between energy, mind and physical body.

Through meditation and crystals, you connect with the spiritual nature of your being. Then you delve deeper, exploring the realms of the mental, physical and emotional through tactile experiences that engage all your senses. Your levels of gratitude reach new heights and it is life-changing. How can you not move with greater grace, and embrace the wonder of life and creation when you take the time to slow down and observe the magic unfolding both around you and within you?

Caught up in the distractions of daily life, we often fail to notice the miracles occurring in each moment. We overlook the profound impact our thoughts have on our bodies and underestimate how our wellbeing shapes our mindset. Yet all things remain interconnected. Achieving presence and awareness at the gateway of our physical senses is one of the first antidotes to disconnection. Now that you

Colombian lemurian quartz

have journeyed through each chapter, I am sure you grasp the profound truth that underlies it all: you have the power to create and manifest your reality, and fall in love with every atom of your existence.

So, how do you continue this practice? I would like to invite you to imagine a world where the magic of Gem Sorcery is not confined within the pages of a book or a set of specific tools — where you carry the essence of this transformative practice, effortlessly and gracefully. The beauty is, bringing Gem Sorcery into the world with you is possible and easy. It begins with a simple act: noticing. Open your eyes to the wonders that might have eluded you in moments of anxiety or haste. Realize that everything is infused with beauty. Once you've accessed certain states of being, you are entirely capable of replicating those states, even in the absence of certain inputs, prompts or triggers.

From the outset, Gem Sorcery's primary aim has been to lead you toward a fresh perspective, enabling you to effortlessly dwell in a state of gratitude and presence, without the necessity for struggle or strenuous effort to achieve or sustain it. The practices you gained can be utilized at any moment. You may choose to carry crystals with you and decorate your surroundings with captivating imagery and vibrant colors; however, as you step beyond the boundaries of familiar environments and venture into the world, where a variety of stimuli surround you — both intense and mundane — you want to be capable of accessing presence and centered awareness, in the midst of it all.

Urban environments, for example, may be entirely too intense or overwhelming for some, but even there, exist moments of pure magic and tranquility. It's a matter of activating your senses to the subtle miracles around you. A bird perched on a wire, a tender embrace between a mother and child, the captivating city skyline, an evocative scent that lingers in the air, or friends sharing a heartfelt farewell at the airport — these all hold the power to diminish negative triggers and pave the way for a life steeped in purposeful gratitude. Because for you, accessing this state of being and mindset has become second nature. This applies to any environment you become immersed in. Even in the most serene natural settings, anxiety, fear and an array of emotions can take hold. What do you do in those moments? You anchor yourself fully in the present through the gateway of your senses. Grasp the crystal you carry with you — a tangible reminder to redirect your focus, to inhale deeply, to feel the gentle breeze against your skin, to absorb the vibrant colors of the sky or the foliage — and you reconnect with the essence of the illuminations. You have experienced profound presence through the Gem Sorcery exercises; now the goal is to achieve this whenever, wherever you are — for resilience, adaptability, wellbeing, optimal health and unshakeable confidence.

BRINGING GEM SORCERY INTO THE WORLD

When I first really immersed myself in this transformative work, I took to the road to seek out the world's most beautiful places, where I could engage my senses and touch, see, smell, taste and listen to their essences — environments where I could meditate and intentionally align my energy centers by connecting to their presence. Traveling with crystals for each chakra, I discovered magnificent locations. Each crystal served as a conduit, linking me to the illuminations. I hiked, explored and witnessed these places with my senses receptive to the beauty around me. I surrendered to the waves of emotions that I felt.

I asked myself, "How can I gaze upon this world and witness its unconditional beauty, yet fail to see the same reflected in myself? Am I not woven from the same thread?" And in that moment, everything changed. I am nowhere near the person I used to be. I uncovered a lifetime of stories and their origins. I created space for myself to rewrite all the programs I was repeating, which kept me trapped in cycles of struggle. The freedom I created allowed me to become a magnet for the changes and realities I truly desired, because my aura no longer carried the scars of unresolved wounds, negative self-talk, unnecessary stress and sickness. I purged the shadows that weighed me down and committed to the illuminations.

I invite you to go to places of your own and make your own connections. Experience some of the most beautiful places on earth and allow their transformative nature to address the years of pain, sadness and self-doubt weighing on your spirit. Though my journey unfolded in destinations in the United States, the same transformative encounters await you, even in the solace of your own backyard or a nearby state park. Your own vision quest can be discovered in various parts of the United States or across the world. Get creative as you craft an immersion uniquely tailored to your own healing path. Let your crystals and your chakras guide you. Connect with the colors and energies of potent destinations, and immerse yourself in these.

Peach moonstone

Throughout this book, you will find a picture of a crystal within each of these environments. I've included the page reference so you can view and connect with them.

◇ **Root chakra:** red rocky terrain where the air is rich with the smell of petrichor after rain, or a vast landscape with oak trees dotted along the distant horizon, inviting you to run barefoot and free towards its perceived "end" and catch your breath at the base of a tree. See page 34.

◇ **Sacral chakra:** wildflower meadows and parks with colorful flowerbeds, visibly sharing the cycles symbolic of art and creation through their ever-changing movement from bare to blossoming, to wilting . . . to departed. See page 241.

◇ **Solar plexus chakra:** woods and parks in autumn, when orange, red and yellow leaves appear as though they were set on fire by the Sun itself, or huge, vibrant sunflower fields in summer. See page 39.

◇ **Heart chakra:** forests in early summer, when the trees are greener than green, evoking the energy of love, compassion and forgiveness. The interconnectedness of their root systems reminds us that we are never alone, and always supported by the Universal Consciousness. See page 27.

◇ **Throat chakra:** the ocean as the tides roll in and roll out, expressing itself like the force it is. Waves crash and then become still like glass, effectively communicating the shifting energies of the weather and the Earth. See page 23.

◇ **Third eye chakra:** natural stone archways that act as portals. If you gaze at them long enough and then close your eyes, you can imagine the beautiful world you would enter if you were to emerge on the other side. See page 2.

◇ **Crown chakra:** mountain peaks and rock spires that climb up toward a bright blue sky, acting like antennae receiving signals from the Universal Consciousness — bringing these down to the earthly realm to be integrated by human kind. See page 238.

As you explore your external environment, you will discover your own natural landscapes that are most highly attuned to the activation of each chakra. The world becomes your physical and spiritual playground, and at this stage, you truly grasp the meaning of Universal Consciousness and the interconnectedness of all. Every single one of your physical senses is activated when you adventure through nature, for this is how we naturally come to understand existence itself.

By getting tactile with Mother Earth – touching, smelling, listening, tasting, and certainly, witnessing – you are entirely present in the "here and now." Racing thoughts slow. Shallow breath becomes slow, deep, mindful respiration. Past and future disappear, even if just for a moment. Stepping into the world with deliberate practices, and motivating mindsets, truly elucidates the timeless beauty of totality and you see yourself in it. Because you are it. Cut from the same cosmic fabric of vibratory light. This component of Gem Sorcery is meant to get you outside, living entirely in your human nature – noticing the wind on your skin and the smell of the trees. Picking up sand and letting it fall through your fingertips. Listening to ravens in the distance. Encouraging your Inner Child to fly. This is your final meditation and transformation.

CREATE YOUR OWN COMMUNITY

To make the process even more fun and rewarding, find a friend or family member who also has this book and set up an accountability routine with each other. Better yet, create a book club with several of your contacts and discuss the ideas presented to you. Call them up right now and create your Gem Sorcery community. Seriously, put the book down at once, and tell your people all about your idea to walk this path together!

Share your intentions and manifestations, journal about your self-discovery, and document the growth and synchronicities you observe in your day-to-day. Schedule days and times to do the meditations with your accountability partner and/or group. Bounce ideas back and forth for how you can all show up more powerfully for yourselves, and for each other. There are infinite possibilities for what you can accomplish. Revisit the pages of this book for inspiration and suggestions.

LIVE WITH INTENTION

Embrace the intentional aspects of the exercises in these pages and incorporate them into your daily life. Wear colors that reflect the energy of the person you want to be. Create gentle teas infused with your favorite herbs, with each sip becoming a ritual that nurtures your body and soothes your spirit. Eat meals that nourish your health and invigorate your senses, allowing the flavors, textures and aromas to establish a deeper appreciation for the sustenance it provides you. Go on a mission to make physical contact with the world — reach out and touch the bark of trees, feel the softness of flower petals, become lost in the intricacy of leaves, embrace the people you love. It is in these actions that you bridge the gap between you and the rest of the world, producing a ripple of energy that impacts you and the world around you.

To bring intentionality into the seemingly mundane is where the magic of life truly begins. It encourages you to step out of your comfort zone and discover how much more beautiful life can be, so you no longer feel the need to escape, or numb yourself, from reality. You come to recognize that life holds immeasurable joy and fulfillment when you wholeheartedly engage with your mind, body, spirit and your own intricate reality. In this moment of self-actualization, it is as if you have ascended to the summit of a majestic mountain, soaring above the clouds, and you realize that this place is where you belong — a homecoming to the depths of . . . well, you.

That is the epitome of all of the illuminations I have shared with you in this book. Everyone is capable of reaching the pinnacle of self-awareness and attaining the non-judgmental acceptance of the ebb and flow of emotions, as well as embracing the ever-changing nature of our physical existence. We are shaped by our experiences and the stories we have been told throughout our lifetimes. Yet we hold the power to rewrite our narratives, to redefine who we are and how we feel, aligning ourselves with our favorite and most purposeful selves, and transcending the limitations of our past.

We are surrounded by distractions in the modern-day world. We find ourselves seeking validation outside of ourselves, neglecting to fully embrace and love who we are. It's as if we dwell in the shadows, a realm of doubt, fear, self-deprecation, hesitation, shame, grief and a pervasive sense of smallness, feeling disconnected from both others and the world around us. Yet, within us, there resides a yearning for something greater, something more fulfilling. What if that "something more" could be found by delving deeper into our own being through our natural senses?

You were meant to engage with your outer world and all that it has to offer. It is not separate from you, it is a reflection of you. It has become all too easy to believe that we are simply experiencing Mother Nature, when we are an inherent part of her cycles of birth, death and rebirth. You *are* nature and you were given the gift to experience it so viscerally. Therefore, it is essential to venture out into the world, and forge connections between your own energetic field and the Earth's. Embrace the spaces where your awareness is heightened. Recognize the repeating patterns and shapes in the world — they hold both energetic and physical alignment with the positive transformations you desire within yourself. Engage your senses, and live in harmony with nature and the magic of the Universe. Get outside to go *inside,* and do the dance of self-discovery.

I've mentioned how I truly believe that wellness is a lifelong commitment, so I encourage you to keep working with your crystals and balancing your chakras through the practice of Gem Sorcery. Continue to explore the incredible energies of crystals and your intimate connection with everything around you. You are part of the miracle of it all.

Pietersite

ACKNOWLEDGMENTS

As I near the completion of birthing this book into the world, I reflect on the many people who made this achievement possible — the people who have believed in me unconditionally and allowed me the space to evolve, express myself and explore various facets of my being.

First and foremost, I thank my mother and father for encouraging me to always be the best version of myself and inspiring me to follow my dreams. You both gifted me with the drive, discipline and focus to push the limits of what I think I am capable of. To this day, you remind me to do what I love and go where my heart knows is right. I never succumbed to limitations because you always told me anything, and everything, is possible — and you were right.

So much gratitude goes out to my husband for encouraging me through this process and understanding when I needed to isolate myself for hours to complete the words you read here. You always encourage my wild visions and abundance of ideas, and make it a point to ensure I know I am capable of bringing them to life. Thank you for also bringing the comedic relief and making me laugh when I started to reach the edges of my sanity.

I want to extend a heartfelt thank you to all of the beautiful clients who have not only supported AmarisLand, but also become an integral part of our extended family. Our shared experiences and growth over the past decade have been truly meaningful. We've cried together, healed together and even become parents together! I am grateful for the opportunity to help you realize your potential. You are the reason I do what I do.

I must also express my gratitude for Fiona and Brittany, and the rest of the Watkins publishing team, who helped me bring this project to fruition. Your patience and dedication has been inspiring! Thank you for choosing me to write this book and become a part of your family.

Finally, I want to remember my dear grandfather who passed away long before he got the opportunity to witness this achievement. You always cheered me on and instilled a sense of confidence within me. I miss you every day, but I know you are here, experiencing this with me ...still standing in the crowd with a big smile on your face, like when I won my town's version of "American Idol". You were the best person.

What an incredible opportunity to embrace discomfort and expansiveness in the ways that I explore in the pages of this book — mentally, emotionally, spiritually and physically. I am certain my brain has transformed since the beginning of this journey, with the learning and rewiring processing continuing indefinitely.

Here's to many more years of miraculous metamorphosis!

With love,
Amaris

RESOURCES

www.amarisland.com

To browse my courses and programs, acquire any of the crystals, herbs, essential oils and other healing tools highlighted in the book, and to discover what more is available to you for your transformational journey, please visit my website.

To download the guided singing bowl meditations, please scan the QR code on the opposite page.

If you are unable to scan the QR code, type the following link into your web browser to access the meditations: amarisland.com/pages/gemsorcery

INDEX OF CRYSTALS

Note: numbers in bold refer to images

Raw rose quartz and
pink optical calcite